7/97

MOBILE

The
KOEHLER METHOD
of Dog Training

G·K
Hall
&Co.

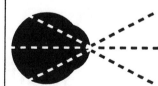 **This Large Print Book carries the Seal of Approval of N.A.V.H.**

The
KOEHLER METHOD
of Dog Training

W.R. Koehler

Illustrated by R.T. Yankie

G.K. Hall & Co.
Thorndike, Maine

Published in 1996 by arrangement with Macmillian Reference, a division of Simon & Schuster, Inc.

G.K. Hall Large Print Reference Collection.

The text of this Large Print edition is unabridged.
Other aspects of the book may vary from the original edition.

Set in 16 pt. Century Schoolbook by Juanita Macdonald.

Printed in the United States on permanent paper.

Library of Congress Cataloging in Publication Data

Koehler, William R.
  The Koehler method of dog training / by W.R. Koehler ;
illustrated by R.T. Yankie.
    p.   cm.
  Includes bibliographical references.
  ISBN 0-7838-1870-X (lg. print : hc)
  ISBN 0-7838-1871-8 (lg. print : sc)
  1. Dogs — Training. I. Title.
[SF431.K58 1996]
636.7'0887—dc20   96-24483

To people and dogs,
especially the optimists
such as Lillian and "Wildfire."

CONTENTS

PROBLEMS

IN CLOSING

ACKNOWLEDGMENTS

My appreciation to the following organizations for their aid in assuring the opportunities that made this book possible:

The Southern California Obedience Council

The Orange Empire Dog Club

The Boxer Club of Southern California

The Irish Setter Club of Southern California

The Doberman Pinscher Club of Southern California

The Pomona Recreation Department

The Riverside Humane Society

The San Bernardino County Humane Society

My deepest appreciation to Bob Yankie for his wonderful cooperation in sharing his training experience and technical skills.

My thanks to Lydon Lippincott for photos and assistance.

To all of you who assisted so unselfishly in our class training programs, I shall always be grateful.

For kind permission to use their photos, I

thank the following individuals and organizations:

The American Humane Association

Walt Disney Productions

Metro-Goldwyn-Mayer

Roy Rogers Enterprises

Henry Schley

Lydon Lippincott

PREFACE

When the complexities of modern living demanded that the dog, for his own protection as well as his master's convenience, be made controllable, the average owner sought advice from the most available source, which was, too often, some local dog-show exhibitor. Not realizing that, excepting a few praiseworthy individuals, these exhibitors were only superficially concerned with the qualities of use and companionship, an unfortunate dog owner would accept the sight of trophies or ribbons as the credits of an expert.

Growing numbers of people and dogs continued to emphasize the advantages of proper dog behavior and when, in 1935, the American Kennel Club instituted its obedience trials, the competition necessary to focus attention on results and improvement of methods was provided. And something else was observed. It was evident that thorough obedience training does more than assure a dog's response to his master's command, capacities for learning and emotional stability could be increased and integrated as permanent qualities of character.

Recently, leading magazines of both general and specialized nature have made the public aware of the trained dog's potential and of the recreational possibilities of dog training as a hobby. Interest in dog training classes and other activities in which dogs are dignified by usefulness, rather than merely looked at, is evidence that the dog-training public has outgrown the "make a game" and "tidbit tossing" techniques that, by not being founded on positive and proper motivations, demonstrate the inadequacy of the master, thus promoting failure of response at those times when control is most needed, as well as contributing to the dog's feeling of insecurity.

Dog owners of perspective have come to want the type of obedience upon which a blind person might stake his life, and to want the emotional stability that is vital to dogs in the presence of small, unpredictable children.

It is to the service of these reasonable dog owners that this material is respectfully dedicated.

From 1962 through more than forty printings, the first edition of this book fulfilled an ongoing need and presented no reason to add material or consider producing a second edition. But subsequent developments have brought about the need for help, which will be supplied in this new edition. At the most appropriate places in the text, there will be references to new situations and help in dealing with them.

The wonderful trio in Walt Disney's unforgettable film *The Incredible Journey* — trained by the author of this book. Bodger, the Bull Terrier; Tao, the Siamese Cat; and Luath, the Labrador Retriever. (© *MCMLXIII Walt Disney Productions)*

AFFIDAVIT

Burbank, California
September 6, 1960

To Whom It May Concern:

I, Raymond E. Shultz, residing at 732 Screenland Dr., Burbank, California, do hereby certify that the following information, pertaining to the experience and accomplishments of W. R. Koehler, of 5059 State St., Ontario, California, is factual.

According to War Department Credentials, Mr. Koehler served as a dog trainer at the Pomona Ordnance Base, and was transferred from that Base to the War Dog Reception and Training Center, San Carlos, California, where he served as a Principal Trainer. Further evidence establishes that in addition to instructing officers and enlisted men, Mr. Koehler did training of a specialized nature.

From July 1946 through this date, Mr. Koehler has served as Chief Trainer for the obedience program of the Orange Empire Dog Club, the largest open-membership dog club in the United States. Statistics show that during this period more than 9,500 dogs participated in the obedience classes sponsored by the above organization. He also conducted classes in tracking and specialized training for that club.

From 1946 through 1957 Mr. Koehler served

as Class Instructor for obedience classes sponsored by the Boxer Club of Southern California. Club records show that during that period more than 1,100 dogs participated in these classes.

Mr. Koehler served as Instructor for obedience classes sponsored by the Doberman Pinscher Club of Southern California. During the period of his instruction, 90 dogs participated in these classes.

From 1954 through this date, Mr. Koehler has served as instructor for the Field Dog Classes sponsored by the Irish Setter Club of Southern California that are open to all pointing breeds. Records show that 140 dogs have received instruction in this specialized training program.

Additional classes, for which the number of participants has been substantiated, bring the total number of dogs trained in Mr. Koehler's classes to well over 11,500.

The following innovations have been accredited to Mr. Koehler's work in the field of obedience classes:

- Introduction of foundation work with a longe line, in conjunction with a complete absence of oral communication, as an emphatic means of instilling attentiveness into a dog.
- Introduction of a system of gradually diminishing the length of a light line, used in conjunction with other equipment, as an

18

assurance of a dog's reliable off-leash performance.

- Development of more widely applicable methods of rehabilitating fighters, biters, and other major offenders. There is no record of his ever having refused a dog the opportunity for rehabilitation for any reason.
- Establishing class procedure which demanded that all class participants make emphatic corrections, and which ruled out tentative, nagging corrections on the premise that an indefinite approach to animal handling constituted a major cruelty. Later this contention was supported with evidence supplied by an internationally accredited scientist who revealed that the use of electroencephalograph equipment, of the same type used by the medical profession, showed that the training efforts of an indeterminate person cause great emotional disturbance to a dog.

Following are some of the accomplishments resulting from Mr. Koehler's efforts in the field of obedience classes:

- The rehabilitation of an unsurpassed number of problem dogs, many of which were referred to his classes by humane organizations and law forces as a last hope to avoid destruction.

- The generating of competitive obedience dogs, outstanding in numbers and quality even in the Los Angeles area, which, according to the American Kennel Club statistics, is by far the greatest obedience center in the United States.
- A record of effectiveness and provision for the physical welfare of dogs that has caused formats and training methods to be adapted by more obedience clubs than those of any other trainer in this region.
- Three of the owner-handled dogs from his Field Classes have become Field Champions, and many others have won points.

I have viewed letters from law forces in evidence of his personal experience in the areas of police work and tracking with dogs.

As an indication of the standard of performance exhibited by motion picture dogs he has trained, three of the number have been selected as deserving of the Achievement Award by The American Humane Association. "Wildfire" received the award for his performance in the picture *It's a Dog's Life*, presented for the outstanding animal actor in 1955. The honor went to "Chiffon" for his performance in the picture *The Shaggy Dog* in 1959. "Asta," trained by Mr. Koehler and handled by him and his associate, Hal Driscoll, received the award for best television performance by an animal because of his work in the series *The Thin Man*.

My qualifications for the above statements are as follows:

1. Obedience Chairman, Boxer Club of Southern California, Inc. (5 years)

2. President, Boxer Club of Southern California, Inc. (1 year)

3. Delegate to the Southern California Obedience Council (5 years)

4. President, Southern California Obedience Council (2 years)

5. Vice President, Hollywood Dog Obedience Club, Inc. (2 years)

6. President, Hollywood Dog Obedience Club, Inc. (2 years)

7. Presently serving as Chairman of an Advisory Committee to the Southern California Obedience Council.

The affidavit in the first edition of this book is dated September 6, 1960. At that time more than 11,500 dogs had participated in my obedience classes. Since that time, more than 40,000 dogs have gone through classes instructed by me, my son Dick, Bob Yankie, and Patrick Smith. Hundreds of thousands of dogs, trained in classes or individually from the instruction of this book, have supplied additional feedback when comparisons were made with "cookie-cutter classes and the on-leash-only" concept.

The criterion in comparing training methodology was always the absolute reliability of a trained dog in off-lead control.

INTRODUCTION

This book differs from others in two ways: It openly acknowledges that not all dogs "want to please" and that some are even viciously resentful of efforts to train them, and it takes the stand that these viciously resentful problem dogs, since they are bred and influenced by man, have a moral right to the training that may be necessary to rehabilitate them.

The book's methods are applicable to those dogs that resist training, as well as to the tractable dogs, which are in the great majority.

Thought by thought and act by act, the objective of this book is to enable the reader to train the dog he now has, regardless of its conduct and character, to a point where he and his dog will enjoy the fullest companionship, and to train his dog in a way that will supply incentive and foundation for later, pleasurable studies of specialized training, so that recent discoveries on the breeding and selection of dogs for a purpose may be applied.

This book has no need for a casual section on the treatment of ailing dogs. Such sections always end with the thought, "But it is better to see your veterinarian," thus what preceded the concluding statement might better have been unsaid. If you require instruction on treating a sick or injured dog, you can obtain one of the books on that subject written by a veterinarian.

The kinds of meat and dry food, which should be fed in preference to canned foods, vary somewhat from one area to another, so there is no casual information that can be given in a book which couldn't be better supplied by an experienced pet-supply clerk or your veterinarian. If you have a serious interest in canine nutrition, the experts in that field have prepared some wonderful texts for your study.

It's probable that at the time you bought this book, you owned a dog you wanted to train. Therefore, your interest and loyalty leans more toward the improvement of that dog than to information on the selection of another. Further, it is a fact that no one, until he has thoroughly trained a dog in basic obedience, is entirely qualified to select a dog for companionship, so the many facts necessary to adequately explain this important procedure are omitted from this volume.

By concentration and emphasis on a constructive sequence of essentials, the author seeks to make the most effective use of basic obedience to change the dog's character and conduct favorably. In addition to providing this foundation, the book supplies more proven methods of correcting extreme problems than does any other volume.

To diffuse interest and effort on advanced

obedience material, which is not comprehensible to an inexperienced trainer, would be to lessen the book's benefits. Further, extraneous material would invite experimenting and "dabbling" with a casual approach, bringing the ultimate necessity of reestablishing the authority which the trainer's experimental attitude had conditioned the dog to flaunt.

Because it proclaims the kindness of adequate discipline when needed to correct a fault that cannot be condoned, the book might disturb some folks who have nothing to offer but their own emotions. Their equanimity can be quickly restored by the device of envisioning themselves in the place of the dog under consideration. Almost always, these disturbed ones say they would prefer proper discipline rather than another, more drastic, alternative, such as being "put to sleep." And it must be remembered that the extreme procedures included herein are advised only in those cases where the alternative is as drastic as being "put to sleep."

If you are determined to use the most effective method to train your dog and believe that comparison is an unanswerable argument, here is a formula for making that comparison. It has convinced a host of "tidbit tossers" in many parts of the world.

With the help of a dog club, an obedience class, or any group of dog owners who have a sincere interest in realistic obedience, arrange for some handlers of untrained dogs to be at a meeting without their animals. Divide the group into two sections: one section that will follow the methods in this book, and the other section that will follow faithfully another method based on bribery or the recommendations of psychologists. You'll need some simple ground rules, such as the length of the course, the approximate number of hours each week that the handlers will work the dogs, etc. There should be no borrowing of techniques by one group from the other, particularly at the suggestion of observers who probably would have nothing to offer but their own emotions. Arrange for an impartial observer to make periodic checks on the handling to ensure there is no borrowing from one method to another.

The length of the course must be stated in the ground rules — thirteen weeks for the course based on this book — and the courses should have as a reasonable objective the ability to perform a complete C.D. routine, including the off-lead exercises. Reliability off lead should always be the most significant criterion when evaluating and comparing training methods.

COMPULSIVE VERSUS INDUCIVE TRAINING

A recent magazine article that compares compulsive and inducive approaches to dog training contains some bad mistakes. The author comments on the methods of Col. Konrad Most, a German trainer of the World War II period, with the statement that the compulsively trained dog is motivated by a "cessation of pain," and she uses that summary to define "compulsive training."

She places me in the camp of Colonel Most. If she had carefully read my training books, she would know that my philosophy and methods do not resemble those she attributes to Colonel Most. She would see that any correction or discomfort I use always follows a period of learning and the dog's demonstration that he understands what he should do, regardless of any temptation to do otherwise.

Following Nature's precept that creatures be permitted to experience the consequences of their own actions, my methods follow the practice of rewarding the favorable acts and correcting a dog when he knows what he should do but refuses to do it. It has been my good fortune to work with dogs in a great variety of training challenges in addition to the obedience training and disciplines essential to all of the fields. Always when a dog's action is favorable, a reward of some kind should be given. I prefer verbal praise to food awards for many reasons, and I always have it with me. And it doesn't spoil.

In training dogs for the behaviors that make them more suitable as companions or useful for various types of service, my readers will see a consistent program of teaching those correct behaviors, praising for each step in the process until the dog demonstrates he understands perfectly what he should do, and then and only then is he made to respond to the command and perform the behaviors he was taught, regardless of any temptation to do otherwise.

Realistically, there will be times when a correction is needed, and I want to be firm enough to do the job, not tentative or questioning, lest my approach nag the dog toward neurosis.

Often trainers who label their philosophy "kind" and inducive will bad-mouth a well-deserved and properly administered correction and claim they never have to use negative reinforcement. There is a common reason for the accuracy of their claim: They are clever at avoiding working with any severe problem dogs.

The author of the article pointed to the operant conditioning techniques of Burris Skinner, who didn't train any dogs but trained numerous pigeons and rodents. She didn't say what he trained them to do. She said Skinner set a pattern of "operant conditioning that influenced the inducive trainers who train marine animals and other creatures in entertaining routines, built on natural actions, toward obtaining food."

She points out the impossibility of compulsively training a whale. It would be equally impossible to inducively train some of the animals she mentions to do things dogs do in their useful relationship to man.

The author of the article attributes "training with kindness and food" to Lt. Col. H. L. Richardson. There are trainers who believe they are performing an act of kindness when they rehabilitate a dog as an alternative to having it euthanized.

As a part of the clinics I've presented, from South Africa to several provinces of Canada, I ran a survey that had an interesting effect on the listeners. I asked them to imagine themselves in the position of a dog considered incorrigible and decide which of two options they would prefer: to experience a severe correction or to be "put to sleep." All whom I can remember preferred the temporary discomfort of the correction to the permanence of death.

As all who read this book carefully will see, it only recommends the severe corrections when the problem has been permitted to grow to a point where quickly eliminating it is the only option to putting a dog to sleep.

But why should those dog owners involved in a comparison of compulsive-versus-inducive dog training spend time on theories and definitions?

We can go to the bottom line and compare the results that the different approaches achieve, in an honest and significant way.

An **In-and-Out Trial,** such as this book describes, would be an ideal place to compare the performance of dogs, although the opportunities would be few as the advocates of inducive training seem to avoid areas where food scents and animals are plentiful. So arrange to visit the owners of what are supposedly the best-trained dogs in your area.

Set up some distracting situations such as a dog might encounter in daily life: food on the ground and a variety of animals that are strange to the dog. The tests should be on things that a dog might be called upon to do in everyday life: recalls, retrieving, and stays near temptation, for example. (Of course, all tests are given with the dog off-lead. A dog restrained is not tested.)

The article is so full of statements founded only on emotion, with not a speck of common sense, that it would be impractical to list them all in this chapter. It is better that you jot down the theories and explanations with which you are bombarded and ask to see proof of the results.

Why not start with me? I advocate my philosophy and method in this basic book and give documented results of one area of be-

obedience class will do nicely.

Here, from the sidelines of the brightly lit tennis court that serves as a training area, we see a colorful pattern of thirty dogs and their handlers. It is the third lesson for the class, being preceded by a "debunking" night without dogs and one other lesson with the dogs in a group. Standing in the center of the class, the instructor reviews the assignment that terminated the previous week's lesson, reminding the handlers that there had been time during the past week for all dogs to learn the actions of heeling and sitting at the handler's left side, in response to a single command, and that the period of instruction in these exercises is finished and that in all failures to respond promptly, corrections are justified.

We move closer as the class dresses into two long lines of handlers and dogs that face each other across a path four feet in width. The instructor tells the class that if obedience is needed most at moments of distraction or emergency, it would be stupid for a member to alibi a dog's misconduct with "he's so excited" when the animal is within tempting proximity to other dogs.

You notice four figures, apparently one male and three female, standing aloof from the other spectators. It is inevitable that you notice them. They're different. They're "wincers."

Your attention goes back to the instructor

havior on page 113. In the case of the philosophy and method I advocate, much of the work has been done for you. This book on basic obedience makes my statements.

Competitive obedience is one of the areas where the result of training can be compared. For your convenience, I will supply you with some statistics you might find interesting.

The Top Dogs Trials, sponsored by clubs affiliated with the Southern California Dog Obedience Council, is one of the most significant competitions in the United States. The average number of clubs that enter teams in the Trial is twenty-eight. A team consists of two dogs in each level of competition — Novice, Open, and Utility — plus one dog at each level as an alternate to substitute in cases of illness or injury. To minimize the luck factor, each dog is judged twice in its class, under a different judge each time. At the end of the Trial, each team's composite scores are verified and compared, and awards are given for the first four placings.

During the decade of the 1980s, the **Orange Empire Dog Club** placed first four times in the nine trials its team entered. (One year the team failed to get its entry form and roster to the Trial office on time and could not compete.) In addition to producing the dogs for our teams, my Orange Empire classes furnished many dogs for other clubs. In the trials where Orange Empire teams did not win, they generally placed among the first four teams in the standing.

The above will show you that dogs that are trained primarily for practical purposes and do most of the winning in In-and-Out Trials can compete successfully in the conventional obedience ring.

Red Arrow Show Girl, the only dog in the world to have all of these titles: Field Trial Champion, Bench Show Champion, Utility Dog, Tracker, and Mexican P.C. (equivalent of American C.D.) This outstanding Irish Setter belonged to the Heists of the Red Arrow Kennels, Fontana, California.

Lesson I

FABLES AND FOIBLES

In the beginning, God created Heaven and Earth. Man, a bit later, created the fable that "the dog, when he understands, always wants to please."

The dog, the world's first opportunist, in some ways knowing more of man than man knew of him, sensed and endorsed this delightful state and was so constant and clever in his professions as to give man scant time to review the theory. Through generations the dog worked his wiles, sincere in his faith and devotion but seeing no harm in throwing man an occasional herring and in withholding respect from those loved ones whom he so easily bested in every battle of wits. So effective has been this strategy that in this day of communication, many books have catered profitably to those who believe they can train a dog while they hold him accountable only for those actions they approve and write off the transgressions with, "He didn't understand — he really wants to please."

Offended? You feel a deriding finger is being pointed at the sentiment so many nice people have shared?

Let's check the "please" theory against the demonstrations of a large group of dogs. An

as he designates the first handler to heel his dog between the lines, emphasizing the difference between "restraining" and "training." The instructor points out that a dog's respect of slack in the leash proves that the handler has instilled the quality of attentiveness, as surely as a taut, restraining, cuing leash indicates a lack of effective training.

A man with a big fawn Boxer steps from a line and faces down the pathway. Before signaling the start, the instructor cautions the handler against the cruelties of light, nagging, unauthoritative corrections that, by their ineffectiveness, condition the dog, physically and mentally, to greater resistance.

"Mike, heel." Without a glance at his dog or a movement of the hand that holds the leash, Mike's handler moves forward in the detached, uncompromising manner of a wave sliding back to sea.

Mike, seemingly more concerned with the uncommunicative handler than with the dogs, inches away and walks attentively at the handler's left side as though charmed by the belly of slack in the leash.

A gyrating pup sees Mike approaching and stamps an invitation. Mike grows even more attentive to his handler. He is inches from the pup. A halt is called.

"Mike, sit."

Mike does.

The instructor signals Mike back to his

place, then turns and points toward a dog at the far end of the other line.

"Faust, heel."

No glance down nor invitational tug accompanies the command as a slender young woman steps out, makes a square turn, and moves smartly down between the lines. The big German Shepherd, ignoring the insults and advances of his classmates, does not challenge the slack in the leash as he focuses intently on his noncommunicative handler.

"Faust, sit."

Faust does — a foot from a lunging Collie.

Six more times the instructor chooses a handler and dog to walk between the lines. Six more times we see the willing start, the dog's respect of the slack, and the prompt sit. Murmurs from the spectators tell you they share your approval of the performance.

The instructor nods toward the far end of the lines. "The brindle Boxer."

A man's voice asks, rather than commands, "Hans — heel?"

The dog that lunges out in front of the man resembles the first Boxer only in breed. In distracting situations where Mike had been attentive, Hans is heedless. Jerking his restraining, overbalanced handler with him, he jumps at each dog that comes into his wild-eyed focus. Action by the offended handlers of the other dogs prevents a dangerous and disagreeable "Donnybrook." Progress on the path between the lines is made possible only by the fact that the frustrated Hans seeks fresh opportunities in that direction. Hans is uninfluenced and even contemptuous of his master's puny restraining.

The instructor seems more concerned with studying the faces of the surrounding people than with the situation that threatens injury to one or more dogs. He appears unaware of a Great Dane's willingness to accept Hans's challenge. But when Hans is within one lunge of the rumbling Dane, the instructor raises his voice above the Boxer's airstarved gasps and growls: "Stop and sit him."

All observers turn the resentment they felt toward Hans full on the man who made such an unreasonable request.

Futilely, Hans's suffering handler strives with the big Boxer. "Hans, sit — sit. Sit, boy — sit."

Hans, delayed by the man's panicky efforts, rears up and mouths at his hands.

"Would you like to pet or praise him?" the instructor asks.

A snicker comes from the sidelines.

"Or," the instructor asks, holding out a small box, "would you like to offer him a tidbit?"

Anger rumbles from the spectators. Obviously, Hans intends to close his mouth on something more satisfying than a piece of liver.

"Or would you like some help?" The man nods.

The instructor slips his thumb into the hand loop and deliberately drops the full six feet of slack into the leash. The dog, preparing to hurl himself at the Dane, is not aware that the instructor has done a quiet right-about turn and has gone, unannounced, in the opposite direction. Quite impersonally but very, very swiftly, the instructor travels four feet before Hans's unhampered lunge carries him to within a foot of the Dane.

It is inevitable that the leash finally tightens and, because of principles of inertia and momentum as old as creation, it is just as inevitable that Hans's flight changes to the direction the man has already gone. Thwarted as to direction but not in purpose, Hans, the opportunist, shoots past the handler in the direction of a Poodle. Even as the dog passes, going north, another stealthy right-about sends the handler southward. Again, the impersonal force of momentum has its way.

Frustrated and furious, Hans turns his attention toward this handler who refuses to communicate his intentions. He rears against the handler, mouthing his protests at the man's arm.

"Hans, sit."

His command unheeded, the handler makes a correction with such force and in such a manner that Hans sits from physical necessity.

"Oh — my."

Turk and Duke, of Disney's *The Swiss Family Robinson*, strike out for the shore. (© *Walt Disney Productions*)

The protest is snuffed out by the vehemence with which the watchers whirl and stare at the four "wincers." The idea that anyone would consider an emphatic correction to be cruel or undeserved when needed to save the dog from future injury seems to nauseate the other spectators. Seeing themselves the only kindly people present, the four fly away like frightened crows, in the direction of some picnic tables. The other spectators turn back to the business at hand.

"Hans, heel."

Before the Boxer has time for appraisal, the handler starts back toward the Dane. Hans stiffens, then his attention flashes to the handler as though recalling that no communication will foretell a change of direction. Apparently there is only one way of knowing what this man will do — and that way is by watching him. You can't learn his intentions by listening, as there is no talking; you can't know by feeling, since there is nothing to feel through a slack leash; and when the leash tightens, it is too late. He's already done it. You can't outwit a handler you can't out-guess.

They are close to the Dane when the man makes the next rightabout turn. Hans sweeps around to the man's left side before the leash has begun to tighten, and he walks attentively, regarding the nearby dogs as so many booby traps.

The dog sits promptly on command when the instructor stops in front of the bewildered owner.

If the attentiveness and conduct of the dogs that preceded Hans was commendable, the seven that succeeded him were as impressive by contrast: Whether pugnaciously regarding their classmates as smorgasbord, or political in their attempts to exchange greetings, or merely overexuberant, they demonstrated equal ability to disturb the peace. Their handlers were strikingly alike in their fault of constant communication, of giving the dogs the initiative, and of keeping themselves off-balance.

The nervous shuffling and stifled groans, with which the watchers accorded inept handling and lost opportunities, subsided. The contrast between good and bad handling seemed too emphatic to result from chance. The ease with which each struggling handler, when he followed the instructor's suggestions, eliminated inattentiveness and brought his dog under control suggested that something other than dog training was taking place. The pattern seemed preconceived.

It was.

From the moment the handlers and dogs had moved from their cars to the training area and until the lines were formed, the instructor had been studying and classifying the people and their dogs, working to prepare the format he would use to prove his point — that intelligent dogs rarely want to please people whom they do not respect.

Because you, in influencing your dog to be happy, composed, and well-behaved in public places, must do some of your final polishing in distracting situations that are open to scrutiny, it is inevitable that you be bothered by overly sensitive spectators. It is important that you be equipped to deal with these eyebrow archers — and deal with them you must, lest you be confused by their protests and weakened in your purpose of thoroughly training your dog. The supersensitive observers are "kindly" people, most of whom take after a "kindly" parent or an aunt "who had a dog that was almost human and understood every word that was said without being trained." They range over most of the civilized world; generally one or more will be found close to where dogs are being worked. They often operate individually but inflict their greatest cruelties when amalgamated into societies. They easily recognize each other by their smiles, which are as dried syrup on yesterday's pancakes. Their most noticeable habits are wincing when dogs are effectually corrected and smiling approvingly at each other when a dozen ineffective corrections seem only to fire a dog's maniacal attempts to hurl his anatomy within reach of another dog that could maim him in one brief skirmish. Their common calls are: "I couldn't-do-that — I couldn't-do-that," and "Oh myyy — oh myyy." They have no mating call. This is easily understood.

When bothered by such critical observations, you will find the most effective counterirritant to be a proffered leash and a loud invitation such as: "Here — show me!" If the dog appears a bit formidable, the "wincer" is certain to hurry away.

Better still, let's use the initiative of a good general and hit the source of the misinformation that they would use to discredit your efforts. Take a look at some of the things that have been written in books and magazines — a really good look. This experience not only will prepare you for evaluating the comments and suggestions that come from the sidelines, but it will also give you the confidence of action necessary for training a dog. The only equipment necessary for this analysis is an adequate public library, a telephone, and a twelve-inch ruler.

"But," you ask, "are you implying that the writers and publishers of these books and articles have no facts to justify the opinions they express?"

Who, me? I'm implying nothing. Just grab your ruler and come on.

Here in a quiet corner of the library, from among volumes on the care and training of dogs, we take a book written by one of the most prominent men in the dog publishing field. Leaf past the pages where the author deals with dogs fighting each other — a fault he attributes to lack of confidence, making no distinction between the small dog who pipes his challenge from the sanctuary of his mistress's arms and the warrior who would smash his battle-scarred head through a window to engage an enemy. Next, dealing with contacts between the dog and cat, the author informs you, again without exceptions, that the biggest of dogs would be disillusioned were he to challenge a cat, and he would surely be vanquished.

Now to a telephone. A call to a veterinarian of any experience will provide information that he has treated cats that have been rescued from dogs. A call to your local police station will reveal that the department has been involved in situations where a preying dog has harassed the cats of a neighborhood. So it seems that in spite of accounts of lucky cats who have jumped on the backs of the right dogs, it is universally known that there are dogs that hunt and dispatch cats for amusement, whether those cats are tough old "toms" or females rising in the indignation of motherhood.

"Everyone knows that some dogs kill cats. So what?" you ask.

Everyone except the man whose book is intended to advise you on training your dog!

44

Beginning with paragraph three of column two on page 133 of the November 1946 issue of *Better Homes and Gardens*, we have a priceless gem for your scrapbook. Mr. F. W. S., the discouraged owner of a "tugger," writes: "My wife and I would be very grateful if you will tell us how to break our Doberman Pinscher of pulling and jerking on the leash when walking. Giving a quick yank on his leash is just so much water off a duck's back."

Here is the "expert's" answer:

"The answer is heeling. This means to walk along by the side of the master in an orderly manner. This is taught by forcibly and firmly holding the dog in position, at the side of the thigh while walking.

"Specifically, the method is to take a firm hold of the dog's collar with the right hand, holding the end of the leash in the left hand. Hold the dog close-hauled against the right thigh as you walk, not allowing the slightest give. Each time the dog tries to bolt, pull him firmly into position and hold him there, to impart to your dog your own firmness. Keep walking, holding the dog against your leg.

"Practice this heeling exercise ten minutes at a time, two or three times a day. It will gradually soak in, and the first thing you know, you'll have a well-behaved dog that heels as he should and walks down the street at your side without a leash. Don't forget to associate the word *heel* closely with the training, so that at its command, he'll quickly assume his proper position."

"But," you protest, "he's got the dog on the wrong side — he knows nothing about dogs."

You're right, both times. Now place one end of the ruler on the floor and you'll discover another thing he knows nothing about. People. Since the collar on the neck of a Dachshund, a Scotty, or a Yorkshire Terrier would rarely be a foot above the ground, holding the end of your ruler on the floor for fifteen minutes will give you a sample of the backache you would get if you tried to train a dog in the scuttling manner the "expert" recommends.

Recently, a pup beguiled people from the cover of a picture magazine. The accompanying copy told of a "tidbit training technique" and decried punishment, claiming it caused inhibitions. Tragically, millions of readers will fail to see the difference between this popping of biscuits into "rote happy" situation workers and the training of dogs in conduct that is favorable even during moments of distraction or emergency — possibly when the dog is not even hungry!

A dog with a liking for leg-of-mailman will indulge his tastes, oblivious to the tidbits that shower as manna from heaven. He'll probably end up as an incorrigible offender — another victim of the "have a cookie" or "shame-shame" shammers.

Magazines have dignified the prattle of "dog psychologists" who would rob the dog of a birthright he has in common with all of God's creatures: the right to the consequences of his own actions.

There will always be more emphasis and clarity to be had in the contrast between punishment and reward than from the technique of "only good" and, if they obey, "still more good." And there is more meaning and awareness of living in a life that knows the consequences of both favorable and unfavorable action. So let's not deprive the dog of his privilege of experiencing the consequences of right and wrong or, more definitely, punishment as well as praise.

Consideration of the above examples, and recollection of other things you have read, convince you that there are ideas expressed in books and periodicals not only infeasible but fantastic.

Confused?

You needn't be. Faithfully follow the instruction this book gives as a step-by-step progression to its first week's objectives and you'll be convinced that your dog is a thinking animal that learns by reasoning from the situations you provide.

You'll understand, too, why he doesn't always "want to please" the characters who belittle him with the belief that his proper conduct will be dictated by previous patterns through which he has been bribed or coaxed.

Dedicate your efforts to a fair trial of this book's instructions for one week and, instead of being confused, you will have acquired the mental equipment to correctly and confidently begin the training of your dog.

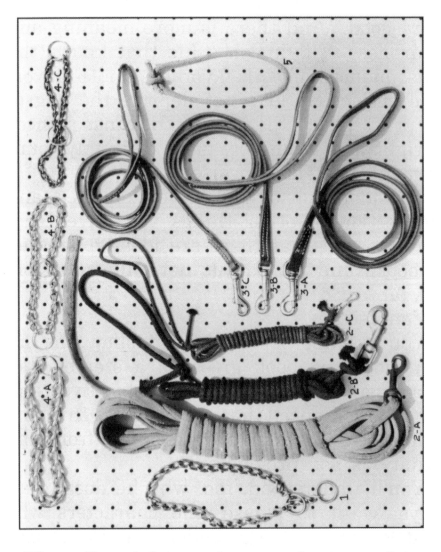

Have the right equipment for your dog.

Lesson II

CORRECT EQUIPMENT

No professional trainer would handicap himself with a short leash or one made of chain, plastics, or other slippery material; nor would he attempt to use an improper training collar. It must be equally important for a nonprofessional to obtain the correct equipment, as pictured at left and described in the following text. Remember — it will be impossible to employ some of the most effective and labor-saving techniques if you are not properly equipped.

Do not substitute.

Article 1. First in order of illustration is the article known as the "chain training collar" or "choke-chain." It is the most widely used of the two types that are practical for training. Its use is allowed in the exhibition rings of shows licensed or sanctioned by The American Kennel Club, which would permit its suggestion of authority to be present in all training and handling situations. This is certainly a most important reason for its selection. It is the type I use and recommend as being the most suitable for the methods of training and handling detailed in this book.

If your dog is larger than a Toy breed, avoid

collars made of the fine, or jeweler-link, material. Buy a collar of the heaviest links, preferably rectangular in shape, obtainable in the length you need. Make certain you are not sold a collar made of inferior metal.

To determine the correct length, remember that, when made into a noose, your chain training collar should slide comfortably over the dog's head yet not slip up on the dog's ears when his neck is bent toward the ground.

The second type of training collar is not shown but is easily described as a band of interlocking, light-steel sections that have short, blunt ends which bear on the neck of the dog. A loop of small-link chain passes through rings on the ends of this band, causing constriction and release as the handler tightens or slackens the leash.

Some experienced trainers use this type collar to advantage in field work and other specialized training. The advocates of this implement claim that because of the limited constriction and wide bearing surface, together with the shortness of the stubs, there is the least possible chance of injuring a dog with this collar. An analysis by engineers and veterinarians would support their contention, despite the views of those supersensitive individuals who regard this collar as a torturous device. It is not cruel.

The American Kennel Club ruled it from use in the shows it governs, probably because its appearance caused the public to confuse it with a spiked collar. If the public once viewed the real spiked collar — a band of heavy leather equipped with a row of sharpened bolts pointing inward and with unlimited constriction — it would no longer regard the stubs of the commercial collar as "spikes." Whether or not the prejudice is justified, the fact that the implement is not acceptable for exhibition is a point against its use in training. There is an advantage in having the same authoritative equipment used in training also present during exhibition.

The most important reason for rejecting this type collar is the curse of its "springy-clingy" feel. It is regarded by many top trainers as a clumsy implement, particularly when making a split-second change in the angle of correction.

Leather slip or choke collars do not function efficiently, and the conventional, buckle-on leather collar recommended for tying a dog is useless for training. It would have to be fastened very tightly to prevent any possibility of slipping during moments of resistance or excitement, and since its pressure is constant, the dog would be equally uncomfortable during his calm, obedient moments.

Article 2. The second figure is the longe. Do not dismiss it as "just another line" to be used in rote teaching. Its length of fifteen feet or more will enable you, if you are slow, speedily to debunk some old fallacies and to learn one of the most important fundamentals of dog training.

Example 2A is a cavalry type longe, made of five-eighths-inch webbing. It is suitable for dogs ranging in size from the very largest (it will hold a horse) down through the small but sturdy breeds such as the Beagle and Cocker. This web longe offers the advantages of a comfortable hand purchase and freedom from tangling. Unfortunately, it is very difficult to find in some districts.

Example 2B shows the second-best type of longe for dogs of the aforementioned size. It is sash cord, one-quarter inch in diameter. Do not confuse this material with variety-counter clothesline, which lacks strength and an authoritative feel. Sash cord is sold at most hardware stores.

Example 2C illustrates a line of the Venetian-blind type, for dogs ranging in weight from the twenty-pound class down through the smallest Toys. However, some of the Terriers that would fall into this weight class would, by reason of superior muscle tone, be too strong for the lightest cord. Be sure, for your effectiveness and comfort, to get a line of sufficient weight and strength.

Article 3. The leash shown in this illustration is the type necessary for effective training. After a week of experience with the longe, referred to above, you will be sold on the element of surprise afforded by lots of slack, and you will be relieved to know that you will be changing to a leash that is not less than five and a half feet in length. Because good training leashes are cut from the tapering back of a cowhide, they will vary in length from five and a half to more than six feet.

Strength alone is not the reason for demanding top quality in your leash. The good, authoritative feel contributes to confident handling.

Example 3A is adequate for the largest of dogs and is also suitable for dogs as small as the Beagle and Cocker class. This leash is five-eighths of an inch in width. It has a hand loop sewn and riveted into one end, and a bridle snap is fastened to the other in the same substantial manner. A bridle snap, equipped with the necessary swivel, can be obtained at a hardware store should you be unable to get suitable equipment at your pet shop.

Example 3B shows the size leash for dogs from the Beagle and Cocker class down to the Toys. It must be just as long but is three-eighths of an inch in width, and the snap is a size smaller.

Example 3C pictures a leash as long as the others shown, but it is only a quarter inch in width. While the snap is much lighter than the others, it is very strong and is equipped with a swivel. This leash is intended for dogs of the Toy size.

If your pet shop has nothing but slippery, improperly tanned, belly leather leashes for sale, or unsuitable contraptions made of chain or plastic, take this description to a shoe repairman or any leather worker and have him make you a suitable leash.

Article 4. A necessary quality of the throw-chain or chainette is the "feel" or balance that assures accuracy in throwing. That's why it must be of sufficient weight and must be linked with rings in the manner shown.

The chain pictured in *Example 4A* is made of a sixteen-inch length of steel links that weighs about eight ounces. It should be doubled and the ends joined with a ring of any practical type: "S-ring," key ring, etc. Another ring links the middle to add compactness. This weight will serve for the largest dogs and is not too heavy for such dogs as the Cocker and Beagle.

The lighter chain, shown in *Example 4B*, is made from a sixteen-inch length of links about the weight of that used in a heavy choke collar. It weighs about four and a half ounces when equipped with rings in the same manner as the larger chain described above.

The lightest of the three throw-chains is

made of material of the weight of a medium weight training collar. It is for the most delicate of the Toys. It is equipped with rings in the same way as were the larger sizes and should be just as long. Remember — the smaller the target, the more important a wide spread of the chain.

The throw-chain will not hurt your dog, so make sure you get one that is heavy enough to handle properly.

If not available at your pet shop, these chains can be cut and made up by any hardware clerk.

Do not try to use the chain before you are completely informed of the psychology that is fundamental to its fullest effectiveness. To use the chain prematurely or improperly can make the attainment of absolute off-leash control more difficult.

Article 5. The tab is one of the most interesting pieces of equipment you will use. It is also one of the simplest and least costly.

Get about twenty-one inches of exactly the same material that you selected as being suitable for your longe. When joined with a square knot as shown, your tab's length should provide a good hand-hold, six or eight inches long, which can be easily attached to the collar.

Any further equipment can be easily described and obtained when the need occurs.

Presentation of the American Humane Association's 6th Annual PATSY (Picture Animal Top Star of the Year) Award to "Wildfire," Bull Terrier dog, for his work in the M-G-M production *It's a Dog's Life.* Pictured are owners Lillian Ritchell and Claudia Slack, trainer and handler William Koehler, and Mr. B. Dean Clanton, president of the American Humane Association, March 1956.

The running part of the collar should go
through a ring and over the neck.

Lesson III

THE FOUNDATION

All is in readiness: You've got the mental equipment to start training a dog and to deal with those who would confuse you, and your dog is at least six months of age (the old bromide to "wait till he's a year old" — and the house has been destroyed — has been debunked). So regardless of breed, there is no reason to delay training.

Your new "store-bought" equipment is all laid out invitingly like the gear of a Tenderfoot Scout on Christmas morning. Like a Scout, you're hurtin' to start. Good. Enthusiasm enhances the capabilities of dog as well as handler, so we won't pull the universal blunder of snatching the dog from the freedom of a big backyard or field and introducing him to training by yakking, "Heel, heel, heel," from the other end of a short leash, thus emphasizing that by contrast to his former state, he's being greatly restricted.

Think and you will realize the advantage of making contrast — the factor that flavors a thing good or bad — work for you. Restrict the dog's liberty for at least two hours before each training period by penning him in his run, a garage, or a porch, or by tying him with a six-foot chain, and by contrast, the long longe with which you'll start his training will signify a reprieve from prison. Cold mathematics substantiates that a dog is permitted a greater area of liberty by the longe than he enjoyed during his period of confinement. Your dog will come to recognize this fact. Why shouldn't you?

The tolerant smile on your face reveals that you find the facts on "the use of contrast" reasonable but not necessary to your situation: "My dog already knows how to heel and sit. There would be no reason to confine my dog and start again on the long line, would there?"

Yes — particularly if you are one of the "oral dysentery" school, conditioned to reeling along beside a gasping, straining dog that is and always will be heedless of your efforts to influence him with insipid, neck-strengthening tugs and the babbling of "heel-heel-heel."

If another dog owner and you were to begin simultaneously the training of two animals of similar nature, and he followed the method of this book religiously, while you bypassed some elements as being unnecessary, a comparison of progress after five weeks would bring you shame. You bought the book. Give it a chance. Do what it says. And, for reasons of the dog's comfort during the period of restriction and training, refrain from feeding him for at least three hours before confinement, and withhold food until he's settled from the stimulus of his training lessons.

Two hours pass. If the area of your dog's confinement was suitably small and uninviting, he'll be ready for a change of scenery, and you'll be ready for the first lesson. Make a loop in the training collar and place it on the dog in the manner illustrated on page 57. Attach the snap of the fifteen-foot longe to the correct ring of the collar. If the longe is accidentally attached to the wrong ring or, equally bad, to both rings, the collar will be locked open, probably to slide up on the dog's skull or off his head, in either instance setting a precedent that induces insecurity and collar fighting.

Remember, I said "accidentally attached to the wrong ring," trusting that you are not one of those "oddballs" who believe they are doing a kindness in locking a dog's collar so that it cannot tighten. Their "kindness" is best defined by their dog's pitiful lack of confidence or his disagreeable behavior in unfamiliar surroundings.

Should your dog at first fight a correctly attached collar, he will do so unsuccessfully and will shortly recognize the futility of steer-like bucking and bracing or shrieking hysteria that is as phony as a lead quarter. Be fair to your dog — attach the collar correctly.

If your dog has reached a trainable age without being introduced to some sort of collar, he will probably be equally unfamiliar with any kind of absolute control, so don't feel remorseful, thinking that a pretraining ritual of "line dragging" would have made things easier. He would still have been unprepared for your assertion of willpower.

With one possible exception you will need no other equipment for a week. You may need some tape to seal your mouth, if habit would cause you to cluck, chortle, or worse: to say, "Heel-heel-heel." For a definite period, we are not the least interested in teaching your dog to "heel-heel-heel" nor to "sit-sit-sit." We are fundamentally concerned with instilling and developing the quality that is the prerequisite of a good student — attentiveness.

Regardless of your problem — fence jumping, laundry chewing, etc. — the solving will be easier if we lay the proper foundation. The most fundamental thing is attentiveness.

We are going to teach your dog to be attentive.

Oh, but we are!

Get a grip on the hand loop of your longe and we'll leave the place of confinement. There is a 90 percent probability that your dog will leave the area ahead of you and will hit the end of the line before he remembers that his freedom has a "string attached." In the smaller percentage of times, some dogs, timid or questioning the new equipment and situation, will be more dubious than appreciative of their release from boring confinement. They may freeze and regard the "go-ings-on" a bit suspiciously. Regardless of your dog's attitude toward his increased freedom, your action will be the same: Start walking toward the area where you plan to begin your training.

Resolve to head for a tree, a stone, or anything that marks a definite spot in the area, preferably not more than fifty feet dis-tant, and to keep going until you arrive. It is important for both you and the dog to feel you have a purpose in your movement. Aim-less floating can destroy confidence.

Quit that — don't look back to see whether the dog is aware of your going, whether he has thrown a foot over the line, or whether he is sniffing or looking in another direction. Don't cluck, chortle, or ask him if you can leave — just leave. Most important, give no silly little invitational tugs that are no more than requests for the dog's permission to move, and refrain from argumentative arm jerks that will change your reasonable deci-sion to walk into an emotion-charged bone of contention as to whether you have a right to move without the dog's approval. The longe locked in your hands, ignoring the dog, just walk.

Shocked at your demonstration of willpower, your dog may react in any one or a combination of many ways. He may brace like a comic don-key, try the line with sharklike rushes, follow meekly along, or snap at the line in a foam-flecked frenzy, accompanying himself with a screaming score that would convince an observer that his tail is fastened to the ground. For you, embarrassed or apologetic, to relent and console him because you think he might hurt himself or because you are unnerved by an observer's raised eyebrows, would be a cruelty. This is not opinion. The author of this book has access to facts on the correction of hysteria, fear biting, and other manifestations of emotional instability that would amaze psychiatrists.

Regardless of gymnastics or sound effects, go until you reach the tree or other avowed objective, then stop.

If it is difficult to resist looking at your dog's face at the moment you stop, occupy yourself with watching the antics of a bird or with studying cloud formations. The dog cannot out-maneuver you emotionally if you don't favor him with your attention. And if he is not occupied with emotional wrestling, he will be more apt to appreciate how favorably his present situation compares with his preliminary confinement.

Whether he immediately begins to enjoy the freedom provided by the long line or whether he elects to play the role of martyr, sulking or cringing, he has his opportunity for a "break." After a few minutes, start to walk again without any invitational glances, chortles, or tugs. As before, head for a definite objective, so you and your dog will both feel you know where you are going. Again, aimless wandering and indecision are not convincing to animals.

Even if your dog is one that really flipped the first time the line tightened, you may find his opposition a bit less violent now. Or, as he realizes that to surrender would be to face a future where you walk and do other things without first asking his permission, there may be a new crescendo of opposition, physically and vocally. Possibly, because of advantages of temperament or previous experience, he may walk companionably along beside you. But though he plows a furrow with his fanny or saunters at your side, do not permit him the victory of stopping you before you reach your objective.

Here, at your second marker, you pause for another breather; then, regardless of the dog's reaction, start toward another objective. You arrive, repeat the short break period, and whether the dog's reaction is good, bad, or indifferent, head down the last side of the square and back to the first corner of your training area.

You've spent ten or twelve minutes moving in a square, triangle, straight line, or whatever pattern your training area offers, with trees or other markers about fifty feet apart. You feel that the period was impersonal and formless — that it would have seemed much more reasonable and definite to have communicated your desires with voice or a short leash. What, in comparison to the more immediately apparent responses to a direct approach, can this method of starting provide? This: For your dog to comprehend that he can only be aware of your actions by watching you is much more important than rapidly learning a few exercises that he will perform abstractedly as you pressure or coax him. By the end of the fourth day's training, you will be convinced of this fact. After a few weeks' work, your confident handling and your dog's remarkably attentive performance will attest to the significance of the method we'll follow.

Back at the starting point, pause, and when you have recovered enough breath to start walking, repeat the pattern of stops and starts. If he was uncooperative, your dog may now be a bit less violent in his opposition or, sensing his tyranny challenged, may scream to the heavens that he can stand no more and that these are his farewell shrieks to an unheeding, heartless world.

After about twenty minutes of walking (or at least thirty minutes, if your schedule says you must do all your training in one period), we'll taper off in the manner that will end all of our training sessions. A correct ending to a training period is as vital as a proper beginning.

Don't jab yourself into a state of induced enthusiasm and hilarity, hoping it will be contagious; don't jump idiotically about as you strip the collar from the dog and, with playful slaps, encourage him to buzz the entire yard in a wild celebration of freedom. This propensity for making all activities fun or a game has done much to confuse kids and to cause mental nausea among working dogs. By repeatedly suggesting to the dog that he's had a bad time and its finish should be celebrated, you will teach him to regard the removal of leash or line as a cue to end his concentration abruptly and dash wildly about. Make this mistake, and thirteen weeks from now, the earliest date when it would be advisable to start your free-heeling, your dog may have the bad habit of bolting from you when the leash is removed. Thousands of dogs have been taught to bolt, bow, and whirl away because their screeching, grabbing handlers had been advised to end training periods with horseplay.

This bolting problem can be avoided. Release your grip on the line at the end of your training session and let the dog drag the line where he will for about twenty minutes.

Why?

Because the line dragging from the dog's collar prevents the situation where the dog recognized the existence of control from changing to a debacle where an overexuberant dog would mow a cyclonic path through people and shrubs.

Oh — so you've got a dog that would scamper wildly, line or no line, probably carrying part of the longe in his mouth. Did you forget? The line is fifteen feet long, and after you've grabbed its end — with gloved hand, of course — during one of the dog's wild dashes, he'll learn abruptly that the freedom permitted by the dragging longe should be leisurely enjoyed as a demitasse, not gulped as a dusty trail-herder's beer. If you are slow-footed, tie another line to the longe before you start the dog's after-training break; the second line must be long enough so, though flat-footed you may be, your agile friend cannot outmaneuver you.

After you've abruptly ended a few of your dog's rushes, you will find him reluctant to chance another dash. A truth rocks you. He is not always sure of where the other end of the line is, so he has no way of gauging his chances of outmaneuvering you. Why, not even an Einstein could figure his chances of outfooting you without knowing the exact position of the end of that long line! You anticipate the future possibilities! And you thought the line would mean physically "horsing" the dog to you and, by rote, teaching him to come on command! Instead, you find its significance to be psychological, part of a situation you can always control by surreptitiously adding sufficient line and encouraging a wild rush. Read and digest this paragraph a few hundred times. It can change your life — and your dog's life. Remember, not even an Einstein could compute his chances.

When your dog has demonstrated that he has the capacity for living at a normal emotional level, take him, again without coaxing, back to his customary place in the house, pen, or yard and remove the longe. If he should flare up in another celebration, don't be concerned. With that dragging line, you've already laid the groundwork for a future booby trap and correction. You've done a good job of starting. Now with the dog off the line, it is important that you respect his right to some privacy. Let him alone. Make sure that everyone else ignores him for an hour or so. The essence of a training session will be more thoroughly assimilated and retained by the dog if there is no aftermath of sloppy commiseration to wash it from his mind.

Now, without being physically occupied with the training, let's review what we've done and why we've done it.

For two hours before the session, your dog was confined to an area that permitted less movement than that afforded by the long longe. Though some dogs may be slow to appreciate the fact, common sense suggests that eventually all must see that contrast favors the longe.

You were careful not to communicate your intentions to the dog by voice or tugs, and so he has learned that if he is to be forewarned of your movements, he must watch you. Recognition of this fact will do more to aid the shaping of your dog's character than any number of responses to repeated communications. This necessity for consistently noncommunicative handling will emphasize the need for a *single* handler during the period of training. Later, when the dog is trained, others can handle the dog — if they do so correctly.

For your assurance, let's justify your firm assertion of your right to walk, should panic or shrieking cause observers to label you "beast." Reflect on the following truths, and you'll continue reassured. While it is not suggested as the most satisfactory method of confining a dog, tying is sometimes necessary. This is definitely true at bench shows where hundreds of dogs of many breeds and ages are restricted to compartments or benches by means of short "bench chains." And bird-dog trainers often tie the rest of their dogs to stakes and posts while they work one or two dogs.

Now concentrate. Can you imagine a person to be more unyielding than heavy dog-show benching or a tree that anchors a bird dog? Hardly. Yet, you will never see a dog that, finding his lamentations of no avail, develops a complex regarding benching or trees. Nor are his yelps evidence that he is being abused. Many children "cry out in pain" for reasons other than physical discomfort. To charge that a person was cruel because his child wailed from a spanking, or a promise of one, would be ridiculous, yet some people seem to feel that the "crying out" of a dog is always reason for imprisoning its master. With population growth putting a premium on dogs' good behavior, training activity in public places will increase and overly sensitive observers must accept facts or they'll wear out their dialing fingers, reporting such "brutes."

Convinced that you are right — that it is not unreasonable for you to place the dog in a situation where he must recognize physical laws — you will begin your second period of training with the great asset of confidence. If you divide each day's training into two sections, your second period should duplicate, from start to finish, the procedure of the first. The second day's lesson, whether single or divided, follows the same noncommunicative, start-stop pattern of the first day. Don't vary your technique, even though your actions seem ridiculous as your dog appears to walk along, burping with boredom. And if he jerks, lunges, or pulls, gather strength from the knowledge that though old habits of the tugging leash and constant talking have naturally made him heedless, he will surely change on the blessed fourth day of training.

So, one long session or two shorter ones, stick to the pattern, preventing after-class hilarity by keeping the dog guessing with the dragging line.

The third day, as you take him from his place of confinement, you may see progress in his more willing responses to your unannounced starts. But should he still oppose you, you will know in your heart that you have given him actual reason to regard the line and collar favorably and have asked only that he recognize the emotionless law of physics that says when he is attached to another object that moves, he must also move in the same direction. So, on this third day, work as before, patient and expansive in the knowledge that tomorrow will see your emancipation — a wrong will be righted.

This is it. The fourth day of training. The day of the change. Oh, but we do mean your dog — the one that pulls and lunges. He'll change if you will memorize these instructions and plan carefully. Confine your dog in his pre-lesson place. List all of the temptations or distractions available to the environment of your training area that you feel would be most certain to cause your dog to ignore you and to lunge or pull. Be it the appearance of a carefully planted dog, the invitation of an open door or yard gate, or a little girl on noisy roller skates, select the one most likely to distract, and we'll begin our setup. Let's say, of a thousand things, your dog would be most tempted by an open gate. Motivated by a background of competing with those who have screamed "Watch the dog!" as they dashed to head him off, and conditioned by straining against the short leashes held by people who chirped, "No-no-no," the gate bolter will furnish action.

Open wide the favorite gate. Prop it lest a roguish wind spoil your moment. Carefully note the time to the minute. Now, equipped with the longe, bring the dog from confinement and approach the open gate as head-on as the layout of your area permits. To best milk the situation, break the slack-line rule and hold the dog close as you approach the gate — just so he'll be confident that there'll be only a repetition of the silly remonstrating that he has so long ignored. Let him be on either side of you. You're not heeling, you're hoping — that he'll spot the open gate. If your dog fails to see the invitation, stop at least twenty feet from the gate until he alerts to his opportunity. Lock both hands tightly in the loop of the longe, and offer him Godspeed and the full fifteen feet of slack. As he moves toward the gate, hold your line-grabbing hands to your chest like a ball-hugging halfback and drive hard in the opposite direction. You should be going at least eight miles per hour to ensure follow-through for the dog's abrupt stop and complete reversal.

And there is a reversal, unless you mush out and slow down. Let the unchallengeable force of your momentum carry the dog at least eight feet in your direction so that the lesson has the maximum significance as well as impact.

While your puller or lunger is still reorganizing, move toward him to provide slack for a repeat performance. The more slack you get into the line before he again heads for temptation, the greater time you will have to gain momentum on your reverse and the more emphatic will be the surprise.

About the fourth time you sell him on the idea that slack means clearance through the gate, you may feel like you've "lost a fish" as you discover the dog has decided to play it the smart way — your way — and be headed your way long before the line could tighten. Now as he stands watching, more concerned with you than the gate; you may be red-faced, but not from exertion. You'll burn as a glance at the clock shows that three minutes of surprise and momentum have produced a significant result, while previous communication had merely shown your bright dog that it was unnecessary for him to pay attention. You ask, "Why don't they tell you those things?" You'll learn later.

If you are one whose knowledge of physics is so slight that you would construe the above technique as too severe to attempt, or, if because of your ignorance you were tentative — thus ineffective — in your handling, read and test the following theory until the truth has made you confident. You will find the example is of additional value in assuring others of the fairness of your actions.

By noose or knot, secure one end of your longe to your wrist. Now fasten the other end to the rear bumper of a friend's car. Arrange with the friend to start the car as slowly as possible in the lowest gear, which will be far less than walking speed. The line tightens and you are eased forward, irresistibly, but without discomfort. Even if you were lying down, the takeup on the line would be so slow as to permit a gradual application of stress to your bone and tissue, and there would be no injury to the arm. But suppose it was suggested to you that, before the line tightened, you turn and run in the opposite direction.

"Why, only a fool would do that," you maintain. "It would be as though the line were tied to a tree. Jerking against something immovable!" Right — only a fool!

Now compare the imaginary situation to your dog's experience on the noncommunicative line. He, by reason of his superior speed, could adjust to the direction of your greatest velocity and your irresistible momentum as easily as you could adjust to the power and direction of a slow-moving car.

Of course, if he were inattentive! It hits you now! Only the foolish or inattentive dog could possibly feel discomfort from this method — and he would bring it on himself. You just went impersonally and rapidly the other way.

If the incontestability of the foregoing facts has blasted the "yakyak, tug-tug" theory from your mind, fill part of the void with another truth. Have someone loop one end of your longe around your neck and then have him fasten the line to a tree or post behind you. Do not peek or ask him how much slack there is in the line. No — I won't tell you to run. A brief thought is enough to convince you that the inability to prepare for the exact moment of the jerk is more of a remedy for heedlessness than the actual physical discomfort of the jerk.

Now consider the three ways by which a leashed dog might be informed of a handler's change of direction: hearing, should your voice or foot sounds tell him of your turning; feeling, should you be so foolish as to communicate your intentions through a taut, restraining line or by little tugs; and seeing, which is the only sense that is dependent on a dog's attentiveness. He can feel you with his back turned. He can hear you yelling with no effort on his part. But, by all that's holy, he cannot see you unless he focuses his eyes in your direction.

There it is. If the line is so slack he cannot

feel you, and if, with closed mouth and sneaking feet, you prevent him from hearing you, he can only be forewarned of your change of direction and momentum by seeing you. Not theory, not opinion, but physical fact says he must focus his attention on you or be surprised by the consequences of the inevitable.

By recognizing and consistently using the combination of surprise and momentum, a handler can obtain a dog's attention; by repetition a handler can progressively increase a dog's attentiveness, thus building a foundation for favorable and permanent change of character.

Back to your gate, and then to the other temptations on the list. Repeat the distractions and right-about turns until your dog regards each temptation with suspicion. Tempt him; repeat the right-about turns emphatically, and though your dog be knotheaded, he will soon regard the temptations with suspicion instead of anticipation. You'll be wailing, "He won't take his eyes off me." Here is a danger point — a sign that you do not realize that each time your dog turns from temptation without challenging the line, he is growing in capacity and character and is being properly prepared for the off-leash work of the fourteenth week. So tempt and turn until you are positive that he takes the strongest distraction as a cue to watch you. Then, hopeless as it seems, try your best to get him to fall for these same temptations, until he's convinced he guessed right — that they were traps and he sure won by watching you. Rack your brain for new distractions and repeat them until, when he is on the line, your dog regards all stimulating situations — the squawking run of a cull chicken, a cat held at an open gate, food tossed by a stranger — as something you have caused and something of which he must beware.

During the training periods of the next four days, increase the appeal of the temptations until experience proves to your dog that the greater the distraction, the more certain you are to control the situation.

Though thrilled by your dog's response, restrain yourself. Enthusiasm and praise at this point can do more harm than good. Between your temptations, stop and let the dog have a quiet break of a minute or two without distractions. Even during the break periods, your changing dog may choose to keep an eye on you. Don't let it bother you, and disregard any characters who say you'll "break his spirit" or "destroy his initiative." Rigid discipline and elementary schooling didn't stifle the initiative of H. G. Wells or Douglas MacArthur.

The attentiveness you've instilled during the first week of training will do more than simplify the job of teaching the exercises detailed in the following chapters. It will make the learning and performance of those exercises more meaningful and dedicated than the senseless mechanics that are grooved by repetition or performed for a tidbit while most of the dog's mind is far away.

Most important, we are laying the foundation for dependability and control during times of distraction, when it is most needed. Right? Or are you content to be one of those persons who stand red-faced in an aura of nervous perspiration, tangling your fingers in the collar of a dog who is "really very smart, but gets so excited"? The choice is yours.

Here is the correct leash grip and starting position.

Lesson IV

HEELING

If you have acknowledged that obedience is most needed during times of greatest excitement or in emergencies, you have used the first week's work with the long line to demand your dog's respect and attentiveness, and you have laid a substantial foundation for the subsequent lesson of heeling. Because we must be certain that each new lesson has a proper foundation, we are going to follow the procedure of testing the dog before starting a new exercise. The first test is easy.

Stand with the dog beside you, close to the wall of a building at a point about four feet back from the corner. As you hold the dog on a slack line, arrange to have someone appear from around the corner, leading or carrying a distraction of some sort. Whether the temptation is a cat, rabbit, monkey, or a bouncing ball, it should come as a complete surprise to your dog. The instant your dog sights the distraction, quietly trot in the opposite direction. If the line tightens before the dog notices your movement, it proves he's not attentive enough for you to start the lesson of heeling on a six-foot training leash.

To start the leash work before you have absolute attentiveness under all conditions will result in a very useless substitute for obedience. Let's go back and see where you got lost.

It may be that you "goldbricked" in your training — too little work or too little initiative in supplying distractions. The remedy for this condition is a resolution to devote sufficient time to the preliminary line work so as to ensure the proper foundation.

Possibly you suffered a mental block on the right-about turns and failed to get underway before the dog tightened the line. It sometimes takes another person's observation to detect this fault. If your observer says that your actions were inhibited or tentative, turn back to the affidavit presented on page 17 of this book. If you failed in your application of these undeniable principles because of a compromising or inhibited attitude, mislabeling your infirmities "kindness," the affidavit will prove you at odds with one of the most extensive and productive training programs in the world.

The degree to which a handler's inhibited thought waves and insecure actions adversely affect an animal has long been known to experienced trainers and now has been rendered indisputable by evidence produced by scientists using electroencephalograph equipment. So if you have presented an abstract, indefinite character to your dog, change.

Or it could be that you were guilty of one

of the cruelest and most harmful of all handling faults: inconsistency. Be honest. Did you handle the dog effectively during formal training periods and then between times permit the dog to tighten the line as one of you took the other for a walk or, worse, let him run uninfluenced toward distractions? There is nothing unreasonable about asking a dog to consider his environment in relation to his master. To assure yourself of the fairness of consistently requiring the dog to think of you first during times of distraction, consider the situation of the wonderful dog who guides a blind person. You may be certain that his trainer, probably licensed by the state, was positive that the dog couldn't be distracted from his task by any stray dog or cat that happened along.

Certainly, a dog achieves his greatest stature and security when he considers the world in relation to a confident master. Comparison will direct pity to the lot of the poor dog whose capabilities are unrealized by a master who can give him only the kind of affection accorded to teddy bears.

Whatever mistakes you made, if any, in your foundation work with the line, correct them and bear down until, regardless of the "distraction at the corner," your dog thinks only of you. Then you will be ready for the first lesson with the training leash.

As before every training session, we

will confine the dog for two hours so that, by contrast, the opportunity to "do something" will appear more inviting to him. For his own comfort, withhold food for three hours prior to the activity.

It's probably with a bit of apprehension that you lay aside the longe and take up the leash. You recall your satisfaction at learning that the longe, with its fifteen feet of length, gave you a combination of surprise and momentum with which no obstinate dog could cope. You hope that the six-foot training leash will not mean forsaking that combination. It won't. The transition to the leash will be a continuation of those infallible right-about turns, with two important differences: With reduced length giving less time in which to turn and build up momentum, the demands on coordination and technique will be greater than when you worked with the longe. And now we are not merely interested in making the dog go attentively in our direction, but we will also start to shape the pattern of heeling correctly.

And what is meant by heeling "correctly"?

Convenience, and oftentimes necessity, in the use of police dogs, military dogs, and other working dogs, has established the heel position of the dog at the left side of the handler. If you have driven a car, flown a plane, or milked a cow, you have learned to accept the conventional patterns of left and right, so if, erringly, you have encouraged your dog to travel on the wrong side or behind you — change.

Careful observation has found the ideal heel position to be that where the dog travels about a foot to the left of the handler with his head parallel to the person's body.

When your dog conforms to this ideal, he will be out from underfoot as you move ahead or turn toward him, and yet he will be within your forward vision. If you should turn right or right-about, he'll be up at your side instead of tripping someone who might be walking close behind. More important, your dog, being required to hold a proper heel position, must necessarily be constantly attentive, which would not be true if he were permitted to slop around in a slap-happy "kind of heeling" attitude.

This principle of increasing the dog's capacity for attentiveness by holding him responsible for accuracy will be employed throughout the entire course of training.

That's the "what" and "why" of the correct heel position.

Here's how we teach it, regardless of your dog's reluctance or resistance.

Because we want to retain the advantages of surprise and momentum, it is important that the collar be on correctly so that the chain feeds from the leash through the ring and over the dog's neck when he is on your left side. (See description on page 60.)

Equally important, your leash should be held in the most effective way. The proper leash grip is shown in the illustration on page 79. See how the right thumb is inserted in the loop of the leash, and notice the exact manner in which the hand holds the leash so that the slack angles across the handler's knee when the dog is brought into the heel position at the left side. Suppose a dog — big, strong, and wild — decides to lunge toward a point of temptation. By simply opening and closing his hand, as he makes a right-about turn, the trainer can release the full six feet of slack and still retain an unbreakable grip. From the illustration, you can see that the handler's thumb absolutely prevents the leash from being torn out of the grasp. After the impact of a right-about has convinced the dog that attentiveness is as much required on the leash as it was on the line and he has decided that the only protection against surprise is a position parallel to the trainer, the left hand can be used to place the loop of slack back in the handler's right hand so that it is correctly held and ready for the dog's next attempt to pull or lunge.

Now you have all the reasons that anyone could want for holding the leash correctly. Let's get started.

By the most convenient means, bring the

dog into the starting position, which is as shown in the illustration on page 79. Then start. With your leash hand held firmly against your stomach, give one command, prefaced by the dog's name; for example: "Joe, heel." Step right out into the leash with the left leg and keep on walking. Be sure not to show inferiority by giving little invitational tugs, nor by looking at the dog as though asking permission.

In the name of the science of physics, I ask: How is it possible for a dog to move forward at the handler's left side if the handler stands looking at him?

In all the world there is no more graphic tableau of stupidity than a handler who commands a dog to heel and then makes response impossible by standing motionless, staring at the dog. Embarrassing, eh?

Make sure that your command is really a command, not a request, and that it is simultaneous with your first step. Again, he cannot learn to start on command if you stand there looking at him after you've told him to heel. You're moving, so keep your mouth shut and don't look back. No second commands, no invitational tugs; lock your leash hand to your body, keep your left hand off the leash, and walk. Yakking, backward glances, and coaxing gestures would merely postpone the lesson that your dog must ultimately learn — **He must sometimes do things that he doesn't**

want to do. So, if you love your dog, let him learn this inescapable fact early and in the simplest way. Whether it goes against your teddy bear instincts or not, it's the truth.

Since your leash hand was locked uncommunicatingly at your belt line as you walked forward, it could never be said that you jerked the dog on the start. He merely had to recognize the physical fact of your going, and he would then experience no discomfort whatsoever.

The results you obtained with your right-abouts on the long line, and which were proven when you gave the dog his preheeling test at the corner of the house, make it unlikely that your dog would try to pull or lunge ahead as you walk along.

But let's hope that he does. It will give us the opportunity to set him right back on the foundation of respect and attentiveness that you built with the longe line.

When he's moved his eyeballs far enough ahead of you so he's no longer aware of your action, merely open and close your hand as you make a very, very emphatic right-about. Because you are holding the leash properly, you have provided the slack for a jolting surprise without the possibilities of forewarning the dog or losing your grip. If he tried to switch directions, you would catch him rat-footed with another right-about. A few of these maneuvers will convince him that it's better to keep his eyes back in a position where they can see what you're doing.

Remember, you can make these corrective turns whenever the dog is tempted to forge ahead — immediately upon starting or after you've walked away.

Again — and emphatically: There is absolutely no reason to restrain him, since no dog, worked by a handler who is familiar with the inviolate effectiveness of the properly executed right-about turn, can possibly pull on the leash. If you wonder why I am so certain of this when I haven't even seen your dog, review the affidavit on page 17. It is quite probable that a few of the dogs represented by the number on that page were as wild as your dog. If you can't keep that left hand from sneaking out and sabotaging your chances, lock it to your left side with a belt. Our job is not to restrain him but to provide the inevitable consequence of trying to pull.

So keep moving along, administering one of the right-abouts whenever your dog tries to forge ahead. Because he has only six feet of slack at the time of your turn, instead of the longer length as when on the line, your dog will be forced to respond more promptly. Within a matter of minutes, his responses will be so rapid that it will be difficult to surprise him. Mechanically, then, you are forcing him to work in closer proximity to

When the dog begins to forge ahead —

Open and close your hand as you make a very emphatic right-about turn —

And drive hard in the opposite direction.

you. The very fact that he is making surprise difficult is proof that he is growing in attentiveness.

Let's reward that attitude with a word of praise, calmly spoken lest it be taken as a cue to hilarity and the thin thread of attentiveness be broken. Then go right back to walking, heading toward any temptations your situation might provide. Continue to head him toward those temptations, showing him with your turns and praise that forging, pulling, and lunging belong to the dim past. *Continue to work him until it seems that no available distraction can affect him. For it is now — after the pattern of response has been set — that repeated familiar experience can make attentiveness a predominant and enduring quality of your dog's character.*

"Well," you say, "it's certain that the right-about can convince a dog that he'd better stay back where he can watch you. But there are other things he could do to sidetrack your program of heeling. Things that the right-about couldn't handle."

You're right, there are. Since it is the opinion of all concerned with the publishing of this book that it is the owner of the most troublesome dog who needs our help, we are going to show you how to stop every stratagem the dog might throw at you.

This will be done without the conventional,

spineless deference to those kind folks who cannot bear to see the dog suffer even slight discomfort in training.

Readiness makes confidence, so if you know, even before they start, where to find the solutions to any antiheeling programs that the dog might dream up, you will be greatly aided. So let's leave the subject of "heeling correctly" for a short time and acquire some of that confidence.

WALKING ON THE WRONG SIDE

Whether old habit, confusion, or cussedness prompts your dog to walk on the right side, the need for staying back where his eyes will warn him against the right-abouts makes it almost certain that he won't move to the wrong side by crossing in front of you. Instead, he may test the "out of sight, out of harm" theory by slinking around behind you. Keep right on walking and, at the moment when the tightening of the leash shows that he's getting well around, lock your hand hard against your body and make a sharp right-about.

This time, instead of catching him flat-footed out in front of you, your turn will head you around right into him. As you turn, without releasing an inch of slack, the leash naturally wraps around your legs, causing the collar to restrict the dog's freedom of movement as well as his breathing. Hobbled though you may be by the wrapping leash, move right into him with sliding steps. This will further emphasize the awful predicament caused by his movement toward the wrong side. He may immediately retrace his path back to your left side. If so, make sure your voice and a pat with the left hand tell him that he's back to "pleasant haven."

Twenty percent of the offending dogs learn from the consequences of their first transgression never to circle behind to the handler's wrong side. If your dog is one of this percentage, he is certainly deserving of some warm praise.

However, if he panics and struggles the wrong way so that the leash tightens, keep shuffling into him. Even if you are hog-tied by the leash, try to stay upright until a chance lunge in the right direction lessens the pressure on the dog's neck and shows him that he picked the right route back. Be quick in praising him for the correct response. If he continues to gasp, jump, and jerk the wrong way, keep moving into him. He's going to try to get out of your way, and eventually, that "try" is going to be in the right direction, resulting in the slackening of pressure and the consequent praise that will point "the way."

The experiences evidenced on page 17 include many examples of handlers with dogs that tried this maneuvering to the wrong side, so I am aware that the leash wound around your legs can trip you and force you to start over.

I am aware of something else — and I want to make you aware of it: It has been a careful observation that three-fourths of the drifters from the left to the wrong side have been successfully corrected by four applications of this "winching" right-about and properly administered praise. And — dwell on this — of the 11,500 dogs trained in my obedience classes, I have seen only one or two that would move intentionally to the wrong side after the first week of work on the heeling exercise, and even these were corrected with a bit more work.

On the strength of this record, I will state that the efficiency of the above method and the dogs' receptivity have been adequately demonstrated and that any prolonged difficulty you might have reflects your lack of concentration or determination. Just let your dog know that each time he drifts behind to the wrong side, he'll cause a right-about in his direction, and the only way he'll ever get out of his restricted mess is to slide back the way he came.

Perhaps you would like to know why we don't restrain him or just repeat the heel command and pull him back into position. That's easy — we don't want to deprive him of his right to learn by mak-

ing a mistake and experiencing its logical consequences, together with the satisfaction of the praise that rewards his correction of the mistake.

REFUSING TO MOVE

Your foundation work with the long line has made it highly improbable that your dog will hesitate to follow you on leash. However, if this new situation, in which you are starting abruptly and with the command "Heel," should find your dog trying to halt the operation by the friction of his hindquarters on the ground, you can bet that his "confusion" is phony.

The subject of "the dog who just won't walk on a leash" is most amusing. Like every professional trainer, I have been brought dogs who were "impossible to leash break." Due to no exceptional ability of mine but rather to the unyielding application of physical necessity, all of them have been trained to lead without difficulty.

Remember — coaxing might hasten a false progress, but it will also postpone, to a less favorable time, the lesson that there are things the dog must do whether he wants to or not.

So don't kid yourself, nor let the dog kid you. Walk. He'll come with you, if only to be near his head.

THE LEASH GRABBER

It could be that your dog moves willingly, even exuberantly, when you give the heel command but grabs hold of your leash and tries to shake or carry it. There is a never-fail remedy for this evil: Lock both hands onto the leash, for maximum traction, and lift straight up. If the correction is effectively administered, the dog should go up like a rocket and descend like a parachute. A dog's second attempt to latch onto the leash is positive evidence that you were guilty of that greatest of all physical and psychological cruelties — undercorrection. (If you are the timid type, turn back to page 19 and read paragraph twelve of the affidavit.) You can only agree that the cruelest correction is the ineffective correction, because it does nothing but encourage the dog to further resistance.

If your dog is one of those individuals who can give an exhibition of pseudo-panic or hysteria when faced with a person who will not compromise, you may find that, rather than recognize the rights of others, he'll resist by hooking his feet over the leash, biting at any part of you or the leash that he swings within range of, thus testing your will and your back. So stiffen both and win out.

"Clear off the ground?" you ask.

Yup — until he longs so fervently for Mother Earth that he'd hardly invite another "lifting" by grabbing the leash again.

WALKING WITH ONE FOOT
FOULING THE LEASH

If your dog tries to foul the leash with one foot as he walks along, the correction is the same as though he were grabbing it with his mouth. And, as in other instances, any of the dog's decisions to contest your will by locking both feet over the leash must be thwarted quickly and permanently.

Since you undoubtedly stopped for your correction, a new start with another heel command will be required.

THE PROTEST BITER

Possibly the heel command is the first one you've enforced, and so it brings out a character streak you didn't know your dog had. It may reveal itself as he crowds in and mouths or gnaws at you in response to your heeling action. However "gently" he might mouth, you may be sure of one thing: To let him interfere with or stop your actions on this first attempt is to encourage future protests that will increase in number and decrease in "gentleness."

When he moves in to protest, shift to a short, firm grip on the leash and give him a jerk that bounces him right out of the mouthing mood. Simultaneously, tell him "Out" in a heavy, disapproving tone.

This is not merely the rather impersonal "lifting" that results from his pawing or chewing the leash. It's a jerk that tells him very personally never to try those protests again.

Probably because, emphatically spoken, its guttural sounds are closer to the scolding of a mother dog, the word "out" is much more effective than "stop it" or "no." It is used almost universally in attack work and other situations where immediate response is imperative. However, if your dog responds to "no" or some other command to stop his action, continue to use the familiar word.

Regardless of how you tell him to stop, tell him once, and then take steps to see that he does.

THE REAL "HOOD"

If your dog is a real "hood" who would regard the foregoing types of protest as "kid stuff" and would express his resentment of your efforts by biting, your problem is difficult — and pressing.

Professional trainers often get these extreme problems. Nearly always the "protest biter" is the handiwork of a person who, by avoiding situations that the dog might resent, has nurtured the seeds of rebellion and then cultivated the resultant growth with undercorrection. When these people reap their inevitable and oftentimes painful harvest, they are ready to avail themselves of the help of "the cruel trainer" whose advice they may have once rejected because it was incompatible with the sugary droolings of mealy-mouthed columnists, breed-ring biddies, and dog psychologists, who, by the broken skins and broken hearts their misinformation causes, can be proven guilty of the greatest act of cruelty to animals since the dawn of time.

With more genuine compassion for the biting dog than would ever be demonstrated by those who are "too kind" to make a correction and certainly with more disregard for his own safety, the professional trainer feels morally obligated to perform a "major operation."

Since we are presently concerned with the dog that bites in resentment of the demands of training, we will set our example in that situation. (In a later chapter we will deal with the much easier problem of the dog that bites someone other than his master.)

First, the trainer makes certain that the collar and leash are more than adequate for any jerk or strain that the dog's most frantic actions could cause. Then he starts to work the dog deliberately and fairly to the point where the dog makes his grab. Before the teeth have reached their target, the dog, weight permitting, is jerked from the ground.

As in coping with some of the aforementioned problems, the dog is suspended in midair. **However, to let the biting dog recover his footing while he still had strength to renew the attack would be a cruelty.**

The only justifiable course is to hold him suspended until he has neither the strength nor inclination to renew the fight.

When finally it is obvious that he is physically incapable of expressing his resentment and is lowered to the ground, he will probably stagger loop-legged for a few steps, vomit once or twice, and roll over on his side.

The sight of a dog lying, thick-tongued, on his side is not pleasant, but do not let it alarm you. I have dealt with hundreds of these "protest biters" and can say, under oath, that even the ones who would appear to be lying most supinely on the threshold of death will get up and walk when a new heel command follows a few minutes of breath-catching, much to the embarrassment of the owners whose cries of remorse were intended to follow all the way to the Promised Land. Again, I can claim under oath that I have never seen a dog that required even the maximum suspension physically affected in such a way that he was unable to continue his training within a few minutes of the correction. None have ever been injured physically. Nearly all have been helped mentally.

And if the dog is too big and formidable

for anyone to hang up? Then the operation must be carefully planned. This is how the professional trainer might "convert" such a dog, while protecting his own person from injury or even permanent disablement.

He would equip himself with a piece of rubber hose about sixteen inches in length and one and a half inches in diameter. An adequate scrap of used washing-machine hose from a repair shop is as good as a new piece. Into this hose he would slide an equal length of wooden dowling, obtainable at most hardware and cabinet shops. Before working with the formidable dog, he would put this "tranquilizer" into his pocket or under his belt, in a quick-draw position, or if he felt the dog was one which would explode immediately, he would hold the hose in the "ready" position behind his own right ear, above the dog's view but ready for action.

Naturally, to slow the motion of his target, he would have to use a left-handed, close-to-the-collar grip instead of the regular leash hold.

As well as he can with the awkward left-hand grip, the trainer works at the heel exercises until the dog shows the first sign of resentment. At this moment (not after the situation has developed into a seething, biting, leash-climbing struggle) the trainer's left hand steers the dog's attempt to one side as a right-hand, chopping stroke brings the hose across the animal's muzzle between the eyes and the nose.

If the correction was humane (forceful enough to be effective), the "biting idea" was jarred from the dog's mind and replaced with the conviction that attack was not worth the numbing and inevitable consequences — inevitable and numbing because a competent trainer, familiar with the problem, would be keenly aware of the cruelties of threatening or undercorrecting such a dog. His approach would express a finality that would end the problem with the first correction. Unfortunately, that "finality" is not possessed by many of the people who have to deal with the biting dog. In fact, a master's lack of absolute finality in dealing with the first puppy tantrum is generally the thing that influences the dog to make a career of rebellion.

The experienced trainer knows that a "major operation" that, by a fair request, challenges a dog to rebel and then convinces him of the trainer's authority is the only way to make a permanent impression on one of these more dangerous biters. This is in contrast to those unfortunate instances where a dog's physical opposition to his master's reasonable demands is met with a lack of decisiveness commonly mislabeled "love and understanding."

Here, by backpedaling or coaxing compromise, the "understanding one" puts ointment on a psychological sore, hoping that it will heal from the top down. By following the dog's dictates, such as not asking him to heel, not touching him when he's excited, not walking into the room where he is eating, the family is permitted to coexist in the house with their "pet," who just needs "love and understanding." Sooner or later, some lax member of the family or an uninformed stranger will touch the dog's right foot, pet him when he's lying down, or break some other rule, and a disastrous flare-up will occur before sufficient quantities of "love and understanding" can be applied.

It is far better for the security of the dog as well as his master when a "major operation" achieves a permanent understanding.

Possibly you might find the process of "absolute finality" incompatible with the sugary droolings of those who prattle that "doggies always want to please," and you may wonder how anyone dares to write such heresy.

Such truths are better written than spoken. Printed statements cannot be successfully misquoted. For example, *the "major operation" is advised in the specific case of the dog who regards the reasonable demands of elementary obedience as sufficient reason to attack his master.*

It is emphasized that the corrections must be made by an effective handler, and in the case where the dog is struck, the recommended course of action is definite in describing the procedure of a professional trainer. To all sensible persons, the handler's justification and method will be acceptable.

However, if you require so much as ten seconds to decide whether it is better to let your dog continue his biting, to always bow to his will, or to make the effective correction, be certain that the above procedure is not for you. Ten seconds' indecision would indicate you lack the clarity and decisiveness to put your point across.

When all of the dog's diversionary tactics (which may range from sliding around to the wrong side, through biting) have been countered, we can get back to the enjoyable process of teaching the dog the proper heel position.

As has been proven, the surprise of slack combined with the force of momentum will force a dog to pay constant attention lest he be caught with a jolting right-about. Since he can only be aware of his noncommunicative handler by watching, he does not dare venture ahead to where the handler's crafty right-about catches him unaware. In concrete figures, this means that no properly worked dog dares to let his head get over two feet ahead of the handler. Caution: Never confuse this natural limitation of distance, which comes from a dog's inability to see behind him, with any suggestion to restrain him with a taut leash. Understand that your task is to supply such strong temptations that he is encouraged to forge ahead of you, uninfluenced by the leash, until that split second when the slack is taken up by the jolting power of the right-about.

When you reach the point where it seems that no temptation is sufficient to interrupt his attentiveness, don't stop. Now make sure your leash is properly held, so as to assure the most effective grip and release of slack, and continue to work your dog in the most tempting situations. When you reach the level where nothing can interrupt his attentiveness, you are taking him past another "point of contention." Continue to work him and to praise him for "not contending," until his attentiveness and cooperation become a way of life. There will be a new feel to the dog's performance that shows that you have not only taught him to walk on a loose leash at your left side but proves you've also added something to his character.

And when should this change come about?

Here's a very definite answer to that question. The author's obedience classes are begun with a first night attended by the handlers only — no dogs. The techniques of combining surprise and momentum while using the longe line are outlined exactly as set forth in the previous chapter, "The Foundation." At the next lesson, which follows the week of foundation work at home, the dogs are brought to class on the six-foot training leash.

After brief instruction on the necessity for the proper leash grip, each handler, in turn, is required to go toward the temptations offered by the opposing line of dogs and to employ the right-about the instant his dog is distracted. Most dogs, having been permanently impressed by their experience with the line, will regard the temptation of the strange animals as so many booby traps and refuse to be enticed into forging ahead. Of the 4 percent that will fall for the trap, only one out of four can be tempted after being caught with two about-turns, and rarely will this remaining one challenge the slack after the third correction.

All this evidence means that, after the first five minutes on the leash, your dog should stop his attempts to pull or lunge, regardless of the distractions you supply.

"But," you say, "the fact that he can get a couple of feet ahead and still be informed of your about-turns is bad — if you turned left, you'd bump into him."

You're right! And that's just what we're going to do — turn left and bump into him, but in such a manner that he'll not be anxious for a repeat performance. Here is the exact technique, as is emphasized on page 107.

Give your heel command and start. Having been previously discouraged from forging heedlessly out in front, your dog's technique will be to ease forward, but not so far as to

The left turn is made sharply into the dog.

be unable to watch for your about-turns. In one coordinated motion, as he starts to ease past you, take up the slack with the left hand and, pivoting on the right foot, turn into him in such a way that your turning step will convincingly thrust, not experimentally probe, your knee or leg into the dog, preferably between his shoulder and his nose.

Understand that the carefully timed moment of leash restraint was to prevent the dog from dodging the left turn and not to prevent him from pulling. Lest indecision influence you to a watered-down effort that results in undercorrection and cruel ineffectiveness, let's visualize an interesting situation. Imagine a dog at liberty in a yard that contains a large tree. It is obvious that were the dog to charge the tree, heedlessly or intentionally, he would be jolted with such force that, unless idiotic or irrational, he would not again hurl himself into a tree. Proof of this is made by each hunting dog that avoids trees as he runs through the woods. Yet the dog's spirit is not broken, though the trees are most unyielding and uncompromising. Absolute decisiveness on your first and subsequent left turns will lessen your task of teaching your dog an attentive, accurate heel position. You will gain in his respect, which would not be true if you were to cheapen yourself as his master by changing your God-given right to turn left into an emotional bone of contention.

Convince him that circumstances or inclination might cause you to head into him at any time and that he'll be more comfortable if he's out of the way. Then get your left hand back off the leash until his "easing forward" tells you that it's time for another left turn. Repeat these properly timed and executed turns until your dog is concerned with keeping all of his anatomy back out of the path of those knee-thrusting left turns.

When you reach the point where he's holding a position that will not interfere with your left turns, you can use a little variation that will make him even more pace conscious. Increase your speed to a fast walk; then, as the exhilaration of your faster gait causes the dog to relax his attentiveness, suddenly slow up and make a left turn. Repeat the formula of speed up, slow down, and left turn until he takes all your walking speeds as a cue to expect the unexpected. So important is the dog's stability when his handler is moving fast that The American Kennel Club has included response to a change of gait in its heeling tests for the dogs entered in its obedience trials. It is felt that even a novice dog should run beside his handler without flipping his lid, though the handler be running across an inviting lawn.

The reason? Did you ever have an unstable dog take your mad dash through traffic as an invitation to play games?

So when your slowdowns find the dog anticipating a left turn, reverse the formula. From a standing start, a slow walk, or a fast walk, break into a trot without invitation or warning, and on about the fifth or sixth running step, make a quick left turn. At this speed, you may have difficulty making an effective turn — you may even take a header over the dog — but keep working. Whether you catch him with your knee or fall on him, keep working until he takes your bouncy trot as just another cue to beware.

In turn, he's been made suspicious of your normal, purposeful training walk and your speed-ups, slowdowns, and runs. Now, as you saunter along, try to convince him that you are much too relaxed to do the unexpected, and as he eases ahead, use a left turn to show him he was wrong. As you vary the formulas outlined above as needed, your dog will come to regard all of your walking speeds as a reminder that a left turn may come at any time.

In each formula, inaccuracy has brought consequences that have made the dog suspicious of the handler's rather dramatized moves, and once the suspicion is created, the consequences and suspicion have been transferred to everyday "noncuing" actions.

In other words, the dog has come to take the very absence of a cue as a cue in itself.

Now as he makes an effort to cooperate, praise him with an enthusiastic pat or word but not in a manner that he would mistake for release or an invitation to play. If he were influenced in such a way and then corrected for his reasonable mistake, he would be miserably confused.

Keep sharply in mind the difference between the fairness and necessity of correcting a dog for being influenced by the legitimate distractions provided as part of his training environment and the unfairness of purposefully inviting him to play and then correcting him when he accepts your invitation. To demand that at his master's command he disregard all outside distractions will build confidence and give control that protects the dog; on the other hand, to direct a personal, emotional appeal and then to correct the dog for responding will destroy confidence and make the dog miserable.

Another question that is certain to come to your mind is that of when to correct the dog if he is distracted by another member of the family. Here's a safe rule. It is proper for the handler to make a correction when the dog is distracted by family activities that are not addressed directly to him, regardless of how tempting those activities might be. It would be unfair for a member of your family to make a deliberate, emotional appeal to the dog which would result in the dog's being corrected for responding. A simple example of fair action would be that of correcting a dog that is distracted by a member of the family who might be rolling on the floor, bouncing a ball, or jumping up and down, so long as the distracting person does not direct his own emotions toward the dog.

Now that you are equipped to correct the dog that tries to go ahead of the proper heel position by pulling or by easing, we will consider the remaining two ways in which a dog might break the heel position.

He might lag behind, or he might veer sideways away from you with the intention of tightening the leash, thereby preventing you from surprising him with a sudden movement. We correct these tactics with the last of our training turns — the right turn.

As you can see from the illustration on page 116, the handler pivots on the left foot as he takes a very long and emphatic step to the right. This is a natural and easy technique to master because the speed of your step causes your weight to take up the slack in the leash with a surprising, irresistible jolt. The dog soon learns to hold a position close in to the handler's side, whether walking straightaway or making a turn.

There you have the technique for teaching your dog to heel attentively in the proper position. Of equal importance, you have the six ways to correct a dog that would try to stop his master's reasonable actions.

If you make the turns in an effective manner and at the exact time needed, rewarding cooperation with sincere praise, you'll find your dog responding with the first lesson on the leash. Work until you reach this high point of attentiveness, then snap the long line to your dog's collar and remove the leash. Release him from command with the word "okay," and let him drag the line around while the two of you enjoy a twenty-minute break before returning to your separate, everyday affairs. Be careful not to remove the leash before the line is attached or the dog might cavort wildly away from you, thus setting a very bad precedent.

For reasons given in the preceding chapter, it is most important that you always end your lessons in the above manner.

THE HEELING POST

Occasionally there is a knotheaded dog, or a dog with a tentative handler, that is always ready to risk the discomfort of a correction that his inattentiveness or defiance has earned. Such a defiant dog will often be made more attentive and cooperative with the heeling post. Correctly used, the device can correct both lunging and lagging. Whether the heeling post is an available flagpole, a convenient parking meter post, or a metal or wooden post you set firmly in the ground, it should protrude at least three feet above the ground and measure from three to six inches in diameter. There should be about fifty feet of level, unobstructed approach to the post on a path about six feet wide.

Let's start with a dog that lunges or pulls and is so tough as to be insensitive to training turns. Start out with the dog at heel on the approach to the post. Do nothing to discourage the dog from getting out of position in front of you. Align yourself with the post so that the forging dog's natural path would be to the left of the post, which is the positioning you want. When his head has passed by the left side of the post, entrapping the leash, lock both hands to the leash by going to the left of the post.

It is now that you might get a stunning surprise. As your dog, aligned to pass to the left of the post, gets close to that point, he might bear to the right to prevent the leash from fouling. In fact, his move could be so pronounced as to push you to the right. Add a little praise to his success as you continue on past the post. You and any watchers could truly be close to shock as you realize what you have witnessed: single-experience learning and the solving of a complex problem when he reasoned that the leash had to be taken back around the post, even if it meant moving his head closer to the post, which was the point of discomfort and which a thought-less reflex would have caused him to avoid by veering away from the post. You've seen proof that there are ways other than repetition that a dog can learn from and that there are things psychologists do not know about the learning process.

Everyone who has thoughtfully observed the heeling-post demonstration must agree that they are seeing a dog's intellect override a learned reflex that would cause him to flinch away from the point of discomfort and rationalize that he should go toward that point in order to bring the leash around the post and thus free himself.

I have staged the above evidence of a dog's reasoning before hundreds of observers at obedience clinics and classes I presented. Often these groups included students of psychology and practicing psychologists. What these individuals witnessed brought forth tears and some laughable denials. And in some instances I received requests to stage tests that would compare theories on motivations in learning.

Two psychology majors asked that I use my connections to recruit a group of thirty green dogs, which would be divided into three sections of ten dogs each.

Each dog would be maneuvered into entrapment on the post, then experience a procedure that would free him from the entrapment,

Use a long-reaching step on the right turn.

based on the learning theories to be tried on all dogs in the group of ten he represented. The number of experiences required for a dog to learn to extricate himself or avoid entrapment were to be recorded for subsequent comparison of the validity of the theories on teaching and learning.

I knew of a very good location for the tests that would be convenient for all who volunteered their dogs and abilities in handling. It was a basketball court where the posts that held the basket offered a good approach and were set in concrete.

Quite a number of curious spectators had gathered by the time we had divided the thirty dogs into groups of ten and had given special instructions to the handlers.

The ten dogs in the first group we worked were gently maneuvered to the wrong side of the post and then shown the route out of entrapment using a combination of soft tugs on the leash, some coaxing and bribery, with a grand finale of praise and a food reward. The pattern was repeated until each dog took the initiative and extricated himself without further instruction or cuing so there was a positive indication he had learned or that no progress was being made. The remaining dogs in this group were worked in the same way, and the results carefully observed and recorded.

Each dog in the second group was eased

into entrapment on the left or wrong side of the post. Now the lesson on extrication consisted of a combination of firm control with the leash, food rewards at strategic points, corrections when deserved and praise when merited. This combination of teaching, correction, and reward produced more evidence of learning that what some psychologists would call only positive experience, specifically, only rewards, no corrections. But the results were not impressive.

The third group of dogs to be tested and compared were worked exactly as described in the first paragraph of this section on the heeling post, which featured the hard-headed boxer.

The first dog in the third group was a mixed breed that lunged into his collar, oblivious to the constriction on his neck. A lunge put him past and on the opposite side of his handler. Without hesitation, the handler leaned forward and kept his momentum until the dog's head was snubbed solidly into the post, then he veered a bit more to the right to lessen the angle in the leash and bring the dog grating around the post. The handler turned around and went back to the starting point to set up another approach to the post. This time, as they drew close to the post, the dog showed an awareness of the situation, and at the point where he had to decide on which side to pass the post, he veered to the right, against the handler's leg, and leaned so hard that the dog was on a new course a foot to the right of the situation that had previously entrapped him.

There were exclamations from the watchers as several repetitions of the procedure showed the dog had learned not to go to the left of the post and be entrapped. The watchers grew more intent as the remaining dogs in the group experienced the same procedure.

After the first opportunity in single-experience learning, five of the ten crowded to the right to make certain no posts came between themselves and their handlers. Five, by reason of timely distractions or more skillful handlers, were maneuvered to the wrong side of the post but immediately extricated themselves by bringing the leash around in the way that freed them.

It was not necessary to check the figures on the three sheets to compare the effectiveness of the three theories on learning.

"Poor Thornedyke," the psychology major repeated, apparently trying to reconcile what he had been taught about a famous educator with what he had just witnessed.

The above comparison should in no way minimize the importance of sincere, expressive praise. Certainly, the contrast between good and bad experience that results from a dog's choice of actions is fundamental to the process by which all creatures learn. It is to remind you that there will be no contrast if he experiences good and only more good as the result of his actions, as some psychologists and sentimentalists would suggest, which oftens results in the death of a good dog that realistic training could have saved.

If life provides both good and bad experiences, depending on a subject's actions, then a realistic training course must reflect the same opportunities for good and bad or positive and negative experiences to teach in realistic fashion.

Before the leash work of the third day is finished, your dog will be getting mighty hard to fool. After five days of using the turn technique, he will be going along at your side, quite concerned with what you might do next, convinced that the praise he gets from attentiveness is much more desirable than the booby traps of turns that result from his lack of concentration. It may seem as he goes along, attentive to your moves and oblivious to distractions, that it might be time to add another exercise to the pattern of his training.

Let's find out.

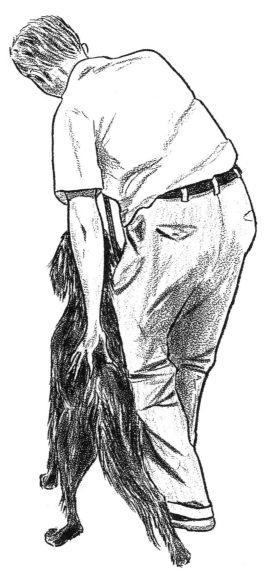

Remember to keep your thumb pointed toward you as you push him to the ground.

Lesson V

SITTING

You will see why the following test is one of the most important you will ever give your dog.

Without making any preliminary turns or corrections, bring your dog, at heel, directly to a new temptation, such as a different gate, an open car door, or a cat in a cage. When you reach the point of temptation, stop. If your dog stops and stands as though wondering what you are going to do next, you've got the foundation for the next exercise. And what is more, you are getting the authentic kind of obedience where the dog responds reliably without any preliminary warm-up or steadying.

Is this tremendous attentiveness and reliability good?

I'll answer that by asking you a question: Is it good to stop an excited dog from running in front of a truck?

It may be that, until now, your training lessons have featured a period of laxity between your first command and the time when you warmed up to the "finality" necessary to get response. Again, if obedience is to have practical value, your dog must be taught to respect the command that starts your training lesson as well as those that come after he's been working awhile.

If your dog doesn't have that quality of immediate response without a warm-up, here's how you can instill it. Many times a day, bring him, at heel, directly from confinement to a new temptation and correct any inattentiveness with the methods previously outlined. Work for a few minutes only, then put him back in his place of confinement until he gets "good and eager" again. Probably a day or two of your demanding response at a high point of excitement will bring your dog to the level where he'll pass the test given above and be ready for work on the sit.

Of the many ways in which a dog can demonstrate his contempt for a deficient master, the "sit exercise" is one of the most expressive. By simply waiting for the second, third, or fourth command or a number of nagging tugs before sitting, he can show his disdain. To add emphasis, he can sit sideways, his eyes and mind focused on something more interesting than his master, who by now is happily misconstruing his action as obedience.

Such response to a sit command is similar to the action of a child who, when told to sit on a chair, flops down on the floor. To say that the child's response denoted respect and the exercise of good qualities of character is ridiculous. To construe a dog's delayed, inaccurate response to command as character-forming obedience is laughable.

As our training progresses to the teaching of other exercises, you will see many reasons, in addition to character building, why your dog should concentrate on sitting accurately. So let's assure accuracy by starting correctly. Even though your dog may have already learned to sit properly and promptly, follow the procedure of teaching the sit as though he had never heard the word. You will gain much and lose nothing.

Since, when you stop with your dog at heel, he stops and regards you expectantly, as was shown by the test, you will find it easy to introduce him to the sit position with the technique shown on page 121.

Here we go. As you walk along with dog at heel and prepare to stop, adjust the amount of slack so that when you stop you can raise your leash hand to apply enough tension to encourage the dog to face in the direction that he's been walking. Now stop. Drop your left hand down across the dog's loin as pictured. Make sure your thumb is pointing toward you. If your thumb is pointing away from you, there will be a tendency to twist your body toward the dog, thus making it impossible for the dog to sit in proper alignment with you. The first job of the left hand is to help keep the dog's head and body in line with the direction that he's been traveling. When he's facing correctly, give him one command to sit, which should consist of his name and the word of command. For example: "Joe, sit."

Immediately, while you hold tension on the leash to prevent his front end from moving out of line, let your weight bear down on your left hand as it closes, forcing thumb and fingers into the loin muscles. As the dog's rear goes down, you may find it necessary to take a short step backward in order to keep your hand in place. The squeezing seems to release the muscle tension and certainly gives a more "unslippable" grip as the left hand pushes the dog's rear to a sit.

The instant he reaches the sit position, praise him and let the left hand work at patting him. And what stops him from standing up? Nothing. Why hold him there? This is not a sit-stay. We're teaching the dog the action of going from a standing to a sitting position and then praising him for that action. So praise him enthusiastically but not with such excitement as to cause him to regard the sit lessons as invitations to excitement and horseplay.

Now give a heel command and, whether the dog is still sitting or has stood, immediately start walking. Go right back into the routine of varying your speed and correcting any inattentiveness and poor position with the proper turn and rewarding cooperation with praise.

Work at heeling until the dog has given you

his fullest attention, regardless of your varied speeds and sideline distractions, then stop and repeat the sit exercises. Immediately after praising him for the action of sitting, give a heel command and work for another minute or so on the heeling exercise, or longer if your dog should decide to argue any points of position or attention. Make it a rule never to follow the advice of a dog who opposes you on a point, believing he can switch you to another activity that he likes better. This is common practice with those dogs that have had long experience in training people and are not about to let the humans take over. So don't interrupt to repeat the sit exercise if the dog is inaccurate or inattentive in his heeling. Wait until he is again seeing things your way, then repeat the sit exercise.

If your dog's heeling was sufficiently reliable when you started to teach the sit exercise, things are going along smoothly and you are finding opportunity to place him in the sit position from twenty to thirty times during the first period of instruction. Probably by the end of the period, he'll be dropping his rear before you can apply the squeeze and pressure. This shows you that the command, the placing, and the praise are starting to add up. But don't gamble.

Keep right on placing him each time you stop and give the sit command, even though it seems that he could write his own book about the exercise. To gamble on his taking the position without being placed is to risk failure of response before you are prepared to correct him for disobedience. So, whether you work one or two periods a day, continue the heeling and placing until you are informed of the proper procedure for correction.

And what about the tough dog that doesn't want to be placed?

Although most "boils of rebellion" are brought to a head and lanced during the long line and heeling exercises, there is an occasional dog that fights the idea of being commanded and placed. Many times this opposition comes from dogs of extreme sizes: tiny dogs that have never been placed in any situation other than mother's arms and have insulated themselves from reason and reality with a baby status which they protect with phony hysteria and screams, or huge dogs, well qualified to resist and conditioned to do so by a master who was told by the dog's breeder to refrain from training until the "bones were properly formed."

Regardless of the dog's size or his temperament, one thing is certain: There is no such thing as "taking it easy," because you are already trying to place the dog with the maximum gentleness. What would be more gentle than the way we introduced him to the sit?

If he tries or threatens to stop you by biting, you'll have to end the argument with the methods used for handling such problems, given on page 97 in Lesson IV.

If you are one of those owners who awaited the "forming of the bones," you may be surprised to find that the dog's muscle and will power also did some "forming" and that your dog is amused by your attempts to push his rear down, or he may just sidestep from under your hand. It is always disagreeable to make a dog uncomfortable when introducing him to a new command, but it is sometimes necessary. Certainly, less harm will result from getting squared away than from trying to pussyfoot around the reality that the dog must eventually face.

So stop with your dog's left side close to a fence or a building. As you place him in the sit, his side-stepping will be limited to a few inches. And if he's so strong you just can't push him down? Keep him boxed in between you and the fence, and put a lot of downward pressure on the rear and sufficient upward pressure on the leash to make his breathing quite a chore. Don't ease up until he weakens and sits. Then be prompt in slackening the leash and praising him. Heel him off and do a turn to which he's particularly responsive so that you can praise him for even more success.

This gimmick of backwashing the success from an exercise that a dog does willingly to an exercise that he does reluctantly or is just learning is surprisingly effective. Be ever alert for situations where it might be used to sweeten a dog's attitude toward exercises that he regards distastefully.

If your dog should resort to panic or hysteria, handle him in the manner described in the preceding lesson for dealing with the "protest biter." I say "resort" because it's a voluntary defense that has always stopped "the master" in the past and which will only be permanently ended when sufficient firmness convinces the dog that "the jig is up." I have never seen a case of even the most convulsive panic that couldn't be cured. Rather, it has been proven that a dog of such inclination as to need the "major operation" is always helped by it, and once the carbuncle is lanced, the dog is always happier.

One word of caution: To approach the problem tentatively, as though the dog's spirit will be broken or his head will come off, is to make success impossible. Recognize the fairness of your objective and win it.

After two sessions of work on the sit, you will notice that your dog occasionally drops into the position before you put pressure on his rear — possibly upon being told. This is true, even if your dog is one of that small percentage which is at first resentful of the exercise. Nevertheless, continue to follow through with the mechanics of placing each time you stop, for to risk failure of response before it is time to correct the dog for not obeying your single command is to do damage. So *for at least the first four days,* stick to the placing, or — if he is beating you to the position — keep trying. Along about the fifth day you may feel that it's ridiculous to try. He seems to melt from under your hand and into the proper position before you can apply any pressure. This proves that he knows what is wanted when you stop and say, "Sit."

You have proven that your dog is ready to be taught that he must sit immediately without any cue except the one command to sit. Remember — one command.

Here's how to teach him to respond immediately to the one command: A few feet before you make your next stop, shorten your leash so that there is about six inches of slack between you and the dog and see that the slack stays there until the moment of correction. This will prevent the evil of prayerful little tugs and will eliminate the need for any preliminary take-up. Now, being very careful to hold that six inches of slack, lock your left hand on the leash tightly against the right hand, as shown in the illustration on page 134. Study the procedure until you are certain of the amount of slack, the hand position, and the angle of correction.

When you've memorized these things, make a stop with your dog at heel. After you've stopped completely, give the command — he can't sit if you give the command before you stop. Give one firm sit command. Don't tug, stomp, burp, twist, or shuffle your feet. Just that one command.

If your dog obeys the one command, praise him, change back to the one-hand grip, and with the proper slack for heeling, continue on your way.

And if he doesn't sit? It has been proven that he knows what is expected, so his failure to respond must be treated as disobedience. Without preliminary, jerk straight up with such force and manner as to convince your dog that prompt obedience is the only practical course.

If your dog is large in relation to yourself, you can gain additional authority by jumping straight up at the time of correction, thus adding the power of your back and legs to your correction.

This technique of exploding the combined power of your arms, back, and legs in a surprise jerk is necessary if you are to be certain of making a humane correction. Any weak or ineffective correction must, by its very nature, be cruel, since it does nothing but condition the dog to further resistance.

If you should have one of the wonderful Toy breeds, don't follow the insipid pattern of trying experimental little tugs. The sit-correction for a tiny dog must travel upward at greater than average velocity or the dog will learn to "yo-yo," skillfully riding each tug without the thought behind the leash ever reaching his rear end. Being aware of the potential of many of these small breeds, I am greatly sympathetic to their hard lot of being "beaten with words" and nudged into neurosis.

The following statement is for your assurance that, regardless of his size, you are not apt to injure your dog even though he is so insensitive to touch as to require a correction that jerks him high off the ground.

According to the records of the Southern California Obedience Council, dogs have been trained in classes conducted by member clubs. It follows that there was the usual percentage of problem dogs which required all-out corrections. It should reassure you to know that there were no injuries resulting from the corrections. In view of this record, if you are inhibited in your handling, don't represent your weakness as some sort of kindness.

So, correct emphatically when the dog fails to respond immediately to the one command. Praise emphatically when he cooperates. By being emphatic in both correction and praise, you create a contrast between your show of pleasure and displeasure that gives the dog an effective picture of what you want. On the other hand, wavering corrections and watery praise dilute into indefinable slop.

If you have done even a reasonably good job, the end of the first period of correction should find your dog sitting on a single command each time you stop. Much can be accomplished by ending the training period at a point where the dog is cooperating smoothly in the heel and sit exercises. This point, where the dog has been taken "past contention," is a good time to praise him and let him relax by dragging the long line around for the usual twenty minutes while he makes the transition from being under command back to his ordinary home routine.

Make certain that you attach the line before you unsnap the leash, lest you permit the dog to spring away from the controlled situation to wild celebration, thus causing him to regard each future removal of the leash as a cue to buzz wildly out of control.

In thinking over your success in enforcing the sit, you may recall several instances in which the dog sat so promptly upon stopping that you had no time to give the command.

The sixth day of work on the sit exercise will follow the procedures begun on the fifth day, of enforcing your dog's obedience to a single command. The noticeable difference will be that now, on about half of the stops, the dog seems to be sitting before the command. Good. You will soon see that you have developed an exercise which, when combined with a bit of ingenuity, can become a tremendous force for adding good qualities to the character of your dog.

One good correction will do the job where
many tentative ones fail.

Lesson VI

THE AUTOMATIC SIT

The test of readiness for the automatic sit is simply a repetition of the work of the fifth and sixth days of sitting on command. Your dog may give you the opportunity for a correction during the early part of the review, but soon he'll be showing the same response that you noticed before the finish of the previous lesson — sometimes sitting as you stop and before the command is spoken. When, about half the time, his action is ahead of your command, you will know that he is taking your sudden stops as cues to sit. This response to a stop while at heel is called the automatic sit. A polling of scores of my obedience classes has shown that more than 80 percent of the enrolled dogs learn to sit automatically from the pattern of work even before specific effort is made by the handlers.

Since he learned the exercise so easily, it is obviously fair to begin correcting him if he fails to sit automatically when you stop. The correction is exactly the same as that used when the dog fails to sit on command. In fact, the only difference between the sit on command and the automatic sit is that on the latter there can be no cue except the fact that you've stopped. No voice. No foot scuffling or stomping. No side-steps over to the dog. Only the stop and, if the dog fails to obey, the correction. If he sits automatically, praise.

As you start working on your pattern of precise heeling and prompt automatic sits, have someone observe your handling and inform you of any of the above-mentioned cues that you might be giving unconsciously. You will see very soon why this is a good idea.

After a correction or two it will probably seem certain that your dog is going to sit each time you stop. When you get to the point where he sits ten times in a row without a correction, you are ready to use the exercise to do some "character shaping." Head out of your regular training pattern toward a spot that will furnish great temptation for your dog. A good example would be any door or gate through which your dog is anxious to pass.

When you stop at this temptation, perhaps your dog may just stand beside you, considering the possibility that you might not expect him to sit when he's so excited.

Let your correction be so authoritative as to convince him that if his mind turns at a point of temptation, it had better be toward you.

Now, take one of the most important steps in your character-shaping program. Correct him with such authority that he will remember the point of temptation not as an invitation fulfilled, nor as a bone of contention, but rather as a situation that you had well in hand.

This, indeed, will be a big step toward the most important objective of this book. Here is that objective defined: **that your dog be so trained that he will regard all temptations, distractions, and emergencies in relation to you, his master.**

The correction made, give him a heel command and go back the way you came; do a right-about and stop at the point of temptation again. Praise him if he sits. Correct him if he doesn't. Repeat the formula. Bring him back to the temptation again and again until he is completely past the point of contention and then keep on repeating the formula until you would bet everything you own that your dog will sit automatically without any cue.

Above all, make sure that you are giving no cue on the automatic sit. No word. No tug. No foot stomp.

At the time when it seems to be a senseless procedure to subject him further to the same temptation, you can revive your interest with this truth — each time your dog is praised for his almost certain obedience, appreciation for a better, more attentive and respectful way of life is being more deeply instilled in him.

A great majority of those who train a dog do not realize the effectiveness of this formula of using the automatic sit in combination with temptations as a way of changing and developing a dog's character. They grow impatient with repeating a procedure that the dog accepts so willingly, and they want to take the next step before their unfortunate dogs have the qualities of character that make for easy, pleasant learning.

Perhaps you are wondering why the automatic sit is the best exercise to do this important job. It is the only exercise, until you reach the stage of advanced training, where the dog is cued solely by his own attentiveness. By not cuing or doing his worrying for him, you are giving him the responsibility of deciding whether or not to be attentive.

Remember this — the decision to "do right" that most helps a dog's character is the decision that he makes himself.

For this reason, it is good that the American Kennel Club has kept the automatic sit as part of its novice routine, against the wishes of the poorly informed who condemn it.

When your dog seems to be enjoying the appreciation of his response to the by-now-familiar situation, you can incorporate a couple of other strong temptations in your pattern of training turns and automatic sits. Work without varying the new procedure until the dog seems to take the very pattern as well as the points of temptation as a continuous reminder to think of you.

Don't quit before your dog is earning praise by working with the relaxed response that comes from complete absence of contention, otherwise you will lose the character benefits of the lesson. Generally this objective can be accomplished within an average-length training period. However, if your dog takes more than average convincing, work until you are successful, then praise him, exchange your leash for the long line, and, with the word "okay," let him drag the line about while he has the usual enjoyable but controllable break before going back to his everyday life.

About this time in your dog's training program you may get an unexpected thrill and reward. Though your dog has been given the "okay" release, and you may have occupied yourself with munching an apple or studying the clouds, your dog may still be keeping his full attention on you. Or, as he enjoys exploring the nearby area, unbothered by his dragging line, you may notice that he is well aware of your position as you stand or saunter along. Here, without the slightest effort on your part, your dog is giving you attention that you were never able to get back when you used to "flog him with phrases."

It may be that you are lamenting, "He won't take his eyes off me." If your dog is one of the hunting breeds that needs lots of initiative or a show dog that should have animation, observers may be saying, "Now you've done it," as they see a dog whose actions seem to orbit around you. Give those "experts" caramels to occupy their mouths until those mouths are opened in surprise as you show them how wrong they are.

You will see that this remarkable attention that you are instilling in your dog is the foundation of the equally remarkable accomplishments to follow.

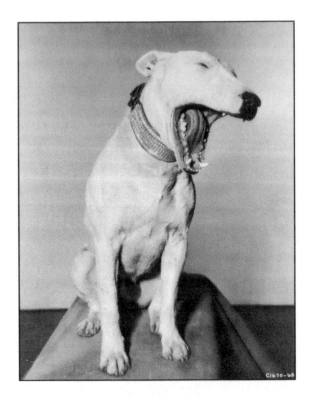

"Wildfire" (in private life, Cadence Glacier, C.D.X.), star of *It's a Dog's Life*, demonstrates that a trained dog is a happy dog. *(Metro-Goldwyn-Mayer)*

Lesson VII

THE SIT-STAY

Before you finished the preceding lesson, your dog was sitting automatically on all stops and was taking your working pattern as a reminder to be attentive. Let's see how well he has retained that lesson — whether your work resulted in a permanent impression or a temporary influence.

Bring your dog, at heel, from his place of confinement. Stop just as you leave the area. If he sits without the slightest cue, he is ready to learn the next exercise. If not, he may need another lesson on the automatic sit before he can pass the test of responding without any preliminary warm-up.

The sit-stay, as the words would imply, is that exercise where the dog, when told to "stay" while sitting, holds his position until another command, or release, from his handler causes him to move. He is no more to be permitted to stand up, lie down, or scuttle around on his backside than he is to walk away. He is to be taught that the sit-stay demands an exact position as well as an exact location.

So that you might better see the logic of the technique we'll use to teach the exercise, let's perform an interesting experiment. Carry a light chair or stool into a room that is equipped with a solid door. Set the chair down, go out and close the door. Now imagine that the chair is your dog and that the dog is on a sit-stay. Imagine further that he is one of those dogs that has been taught that breaking from a stay position will bring nothing more than a repetition of the command. How would you know when to repeat the command?

"That's a stupid question," you say. "You wouldn't know when to repeat the command unless you could see him, and you can't see a dog through solid walls."

You're so right. What you are admitting is that a stay which a dog holds only when constantly reminded or threatened is useless when the handler is out of sight.

Perhaps you would prefer the useful sit-stay — the type that will control a dog whether the handler is in sight or out of sight. If so, you must start right. And "right" bears no resemblance to the common, pathetic routine of starting the command by pushing the dog back as he moves from position, and repeating, "Stay, stay, stay, stay," while you shake your finger at him.

Instead, we are going to introduce the dog to the sit-stay by a method that will encourage him to resist temptation from the beginning.

The technique of teaching the sit-stay is a series of mechanical steps that must be followed exactly as described if you and your dog are to progress with a smooth confidence. If you have difficulty using written instructions, read, and rehearse these steps without your dog until the order of procedure is sharp in your mind.

First, just before making a routine stop, reduce the amount of slack to about ten inches. After you've stopped and your dog has sat automatically, raise your right hand smoothly, *without* jerking, to apply sufficient tension to encourage the dog to remain seated. (See illustration on page 144.) Next, give a command — "Joe, stay" — and as you speak, extend your left hand, fingers fully spread, to a position a few inches in front of your dog's face. Hold that hand in position as you take a single step with the right foot, pivoting on the left foot toward the dog, so that you are facing the dog from a location one step in front of him. (The illustration on page 145 diagrams this pivoting step.) While the leash should not be vertical as when making an actual sit correction, the tension should be at such an angle as to encourage the dog to remain seated, rather than to move toward you.

It is known that animals sometimes instinctively understand positive gestures, and you may be pleased to see your dog regard your extended left hand as if he knows what you want.

Now, as you continue to hold that left-hand

Tell the dog to stay before you take the
pivoting step in front of him.

Keep the correct angle on the leash.

gesture, without letting the tension go completely out of the leash, increase and decrease the pressure in a series of weak, unemphatic tugs, which, because of previous experience in sitting, your dog is certain to resist. Also, the angle is such that the dog would have to defy gravity in order to move in the direction of the tension, so he could hardly do other than resist those unauthoritative little tugs.

Now with the restraining tension still in the leash, reverse your pivoting step so that it puts you back in your position at the dog's side. Release the tension in the leash and lower the left hand to pat the dog as you praise him for resisting the temptation of your movements and the tugs on the leash. The exercise finished, heel him back into your pattern of work.

About one dog owner in a hundred will experience difficulty in starting the sit-stay. That person will be one of two types. He will be one of the "kindlies" who has practiced pussyfooting around his dog's showings of disrespect, believing that some miracle will change his own status from that of a doormat to that of the dog's master. His dog, true to form, may lunge in any direction, hook his feet over the leash, or try one of the other "brat routines" that no properly disciplined dog would dare attempt. The correction is almost the same as that recommended for controlling the dog that rears and paws when the heeling exercise is started. Grant him his wish to become "airborne," keep him elevated until he has neither the strength nor the will for further rebellion, and when at last, with grateful heart, he is returned to earth, keep the angle of the leash so steep that sitting, not moving, will be uppermost in his mind.

The other type of dog owner that is apt to have trouble with the sit-stay is the "carrier type." This type generally owns a small dog, often a Poodle, that has been picked up on dozens of excuses, ranging from a cold pavement to the owner's teddy-bear complex. This dog regards everything in the way of word and gesture as an invitation "to arms," and the left hand position and leash tension are sure to find him standing on his hind legs, front paws outstretched in anticipation.

To correct this problem, keep the tension straight up, so that the dog cannot move toward you but finally dangles back to the sit position. If he should panic, as is often the case with those dogs that have been shielded from reality, the panic can best be drained off by slowing the "dangle." If the "dangle" is slow enough, the panic will not recur. Be consistent and he'll soon realize that he's more comfortable when his rear is on the ground. From then on, he can be handled on the sit-stay as easily as a dog that has lived in a favorable environment.

During this first period of work on the

sit-stay, you will probably repeat the exercise at least fifteen times. Within the training time of the next three days, your dog, if effectively worked, will understand his obligation on the sit-stay and it will be time to correct any disobedience to the stay command.

Naturally, since training in reliable obedience can best be done in situations which the trainer sets up or rigs to his own advantage — never by a catch-him-if-you-can method — you must get the dog to disobey in a situation that you can control.

Start the training period of the fourth day by reviewing the exercises of heeling, sitting automatically, and the start of the sit-stay. Then, on about the fourth automatic sit, give the usual stay command and hand gesture as you put tension on the leash and take that pivoting step that puts you in front of and facing the dog. Remember — give the command as you leave, not after. Now, release the tension by letting the full amount of slack come into the leash. Be certain to keep an unbreakable grip on the hand loop. With that belly of slack in the leash, take another step straight backward, which will put you four or five feet from your dog.

There are two things to remember about the stay command — give it before you leave, not after, and then keep your mouth shut.

Furthermore, since you have given him a hand signal to stay, you can relax that left hand and let the dog do all the "remembering" about the command.

Possibly you did such a good job of acquainting your dog with the meaning of the stay command that he seems to comprehend he should stay, even though you are five feet away and nothing is restraining him.

To ask him to hold for more than five seconds on this first trial is possibly to miss an opportunity to reward him for his good judgment, so retrace your steps, pivot back to position at his side, and praise him.

Be certain not to let the dog use the action of your return nor your praise as an excuse to move before the exercise is finished. Now, end the exercise with a heel command and start back into your working pattern of heeling and automatic sits.

By returning and praising the dog after he held even for such a short time, you will eliminate the possibility of confusion and give the dog an important feeling of accomplishment — showing him that he was right in believing that even though you stepped back farther than usual, he did right to stay.

And what if he didn't stay but — tempted by the new situation — moved before the five seconds elapsed, when you praised him, or before your heel command ended the exercise?

In any case, keep your mouth shut and move very fast toward the spot where your dog

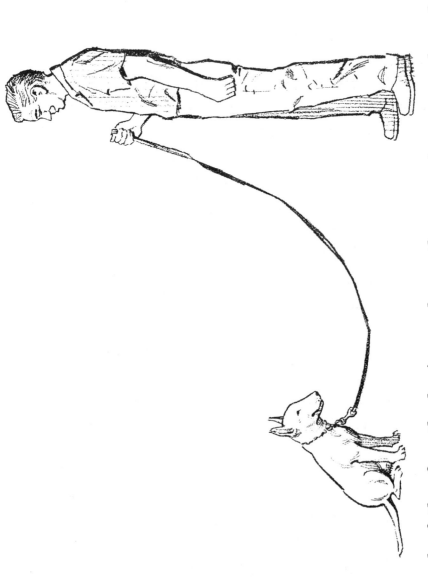

By the end of the fourth day's work on the exercise, your dog should hold for five seconds with the handler several feet in front of him.

should have stayed sitting. As you move, gather the slack with your free hand so you will have just enough to take up with a two-handed corrective jerk that propels — not leads — the dog back to his proper position.

You will not be confused, nor confuse your dog, if you remember that the correction should jerk the dog from where he moved back to where he should be and that the path of the correction should be the exact reverse of the pattern the dog followed when he moved. It is vitally important that the correction be in the direction from whence the dog broke. This rule applies whether the dog broke when you were out in front or when you returned to his side.

People of normal intelligence are aware that a dog generally moves because he wants to, and for a trainer to merely lead him back to where he was left and to tell him to stay would result in a reward not a correction. So, if you are one of those who would lead or push the dog back and then repeat the word "stay," the chances are you will be regarded as quite a curiosity.

Whether your dog comprehended from the first that the new situation, with more distance and a slack leash, would be no excuse for moving, or required many corrections to convince him that "stay" meant "stay," regardless of your position, when he has held several consecutive times for at least five seconds, it

After seven days on the exercise, return to the dog using the counterclockwise pattern as shown.

will be apparent that he understands his obligation and is ready for a program of stability-building temptations.

The second day's training, after you have started the stay corrections, will begin with a review of your pattern of exercises. Work on heeling, the automatic sit, and the sit-stay. When your dog has held two sit-stays for five seconds each, begin to lengthen the period you remain standing in front of him. Progress from five seconds to longer periods, using properly timed and applied praise and corrections until, by the end of the session, your dog will stay for at least a half minute with you standing a loose leash-length in front of him. Remember — the word was "progress," not "jump." Gradually increase the time.

Proper timing is vital to your success with the stay exercises. After making a correction, insist that the dog hold his position until you finish the exercise. Your responsibility is to watch for any sign of willingness or resignation that shows your dog is ready to cooperate and to get back and show him with praise that his change of viewpoint is a good thing for both of you.

To get full benefit from your corrections and to avoid confusing the dog, make this your rule: Following any correction, take the dog's first sign of cooperation as the moment to return and praise him for proper response.

You might wonder why, if the "break" and

correction came after only a few seconds of the exercise, the dog's quick change of heart should merit praise instead of a demand that he finish out the rest of an average period.

There is good reason. If the dog were honestly confused and in doubt as to the proper action, your prompt appreciation would show him that he had made the right decision. This opportunity might be lost if you required him to hold past the first sign of willingness after the correction. There is nothing inconsistent in your action because, should he move as you return to praise him or break when you again leave him, he will again be corrected. If your correction and praise are the inevitable results of his own actions, his resistance to time and other temptations will grow naturally.

However, if you have a tough and cagey dog that you know deliberately breaks a stay, taking the correction so that he can earn praise and quick release by holding only a short stay, you'll have to outmaneuver him by making him extend his brief periods of willingness into longer periods. He'll quickly figure out that he'd just as well hold the required length of time when he's first told to stay, because the period that follows the correction will be just as long as the first period you had planned.

Continue to lengthen the stay periods until, by the end of the sixth day's work on the exercise, you will be requiring the dog to hold as you stand a leash-length in front of him for a full minute.

Though the average dog easily reaches this goal of minute stays by the end of the sixth day's training, there is some variation in the rate of progress between individual dogs. When your dog has held the minute sit-stay five times in a row, you'll know that you are prepared to add another temptation. This is the temptation of motion.

The next training period, after you've proven your dog's readiness, should begin with the customary review of all exercises to date. The third time you face him on a stay, take a step to the right. Next, take a step back to the left. Reverse the order by taking a step to the left and then back to the right. If your dog holds in the face of this distracting motion, return to praise him and finish the exercise. If he doesn't want to hold, follow through with corrections until he does.

Work on heeling and sitting for a minute or two, then do another stay. This time add a forward and backward step to the pattern of sidesteps. After consistent praise and correction has taught your dog to ignore your steps, try dropping on one knee, sitting on the ground in front of him, then jumping up and down. On all of your movements, be careful not to jerk on the leash.

Any tempting activity in which you might

engage, from standing on your head to frying hamburgers in front of him, is fair temptation so long as it is not personally addressed to your dog. Quite probably, in everyday life with your dog, you will sometime have to make a fast or exciting move while he holds a stay. Certainly, if your dog is to be with you as a pal, there will be times when you will want him to stay while you or others eat. No, there is nothing unfair about asking your dog to be obedient in the exciting situations where obedience is most needed.

Having convinced your dog with praise and correction that your stepping, kneeling, and jumping are not an invitation for him to move, you will be prepared to start a new route of returning to your dog from your position out in front.

From now on, as you return to your dog when he has been left on a stay, walk back in a counterclockwise pattern that takes you past the dog's left side, around behind him, and up to a stop beside him so that you are standing with the dog in a heel position at your left side, ready for the heel command that ends the stay. Don't circle widely as you return in the new counterclockwise pattern. This could confuse the dog by causing a pull sideways. Let the leash hang freely from your left hand as you return in the manner illustrated. Gather the leash up only as you give the heel command that ends the exercise.

If he holds from start to finish, praise him and finish the exercise. If he breaks from the position, correct him. And remember — it is a break of position if he lies down, stands, or scoots or pivots on his backside in order to watch as you move around him. It's all right for him to swivel his head around a bit, providing his feet do not move. Don't forget — the correction should always oppose the direction of the dog's movement. For example, if he spins to the left, your jerk should spin him to the right, back to his starting position.

The often-made mistake of spinning a dog completely around, back to position, in the direction that he had chosen to break instead of back the way he came, can delay progress in getting your dog to hold solidly as you return to finish the stay exercises.

We've been concentrating mostly on your dog's performance and how to control it. Let's take a look at yours. It may be that you are guilty of that common blunder of stepping away from your dog and then telling him to stay. Though the procedure sounds a bit insane, it is not unusual for a trainer to work at teaching his dog to hold on one stay command and then forget his own obligation to give that command before, not after, he leaves. In the name of fairness and common sense, give the command and gesture just before you leave, not after you've gone. And do your stepping away on the right foot, instead of the left foot, for association has taught the dog to take your stepping away on your left foot as a cue to heel.

Before you start waving a rule book, let me assure you that I am well aware that my instruction to use both the dog's name and the word "stay" in combination with a hand signal is incompatible with the American Kennel Club's rule for leaving a dog on a stay in an obedience trial. I am also aware of some other things relative to the teaching of the stay commands. I know, for example, that dogs are instinctively comprehensive of hand signals on the stay exercise. When used in combination with the verbal command, they can do much to endow the word with meaning, to assure emphasis and clarity of command so often lacking in amateur handling, as well as to lay the foundation for future use of hand signals should your success inspire you to the challenge of advanced training. You will find that once your dog is solid on his stays, it's an easy task to conform with the rules. Until then, make your teaching job easier by using the combination command as described above.

When you are certain that you know how to leave a dog on the stay, to correct if he disobeys as well as to return to him properly, and your dog holds consistently for as long as three minutes, you are prepared to commit the exercise to your training pattern for further perfecting along with the other exercises.

To avoid confusing you and your dog and to assure the correct foundation for each successive training step, we have dealt with the exercises singly and in the most effective order, and have developed each to a reasonable degree of noncontention before turning attention to the learning of something new. My constant reference to "the pattern of your work" should indicate that each exercise as it is learned should be committed to that training pattern for further development. By practicing obedience, your dog will become ever more happily adjusted to an obedient way of life.

Your pattern of work will divide time equally between the exercises except in instances where a dog's confusion or reluctance indicates that an exercise needs more than average effort.

Do not let the dog's obstinacy deflect your efforts from an exercise he dislikes to another he does willingly. Stay with each bone of contention until you've won your point and can praise him for cooperation. Then go to another exercise. The sometimes recommended technique of sneaking around an exercise has never helped a human or his dog. If you quit before you resolve an issue, your dog will know you for what you are — a quitter.

In a later chapter, after all basic exercises have been learned, they will be studied and developed with an eye to extending reliability and usefulness. So, when you are certain that you and your dog each know what is supposed to be done on the sit-stay, add the exercise to the heel and sit, for the benefits of practice, and we'll turn to the learning of something new.

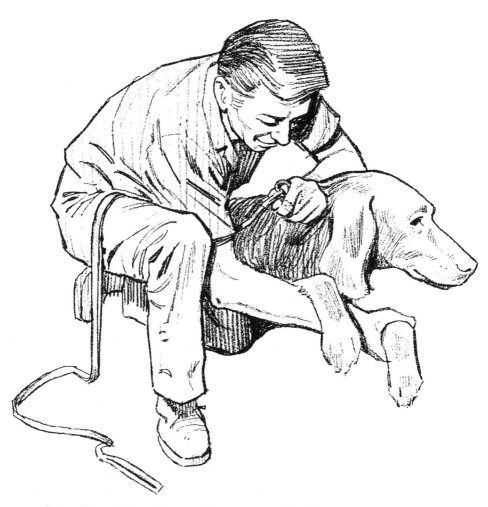

Study this drawing carefully.

Lesson VIII

THE DOWN

You may have seen the method of starting a dog on the "down" exercise through forcing his head toward the ground by means of the trainer's foot on the leash. There are many ways in which this technique is unfair to the trainer and the dog. Count them.

First of all, a dog's attitude toward the down is not going to be one of willingness if his first association with the command is the pain of being strangled into a position that he does not understand.

Confused, as he probably will be, by the strange position and unfamiliar request, he is very apt to rebel — and rebel successfully, for this is no pull forward to make him walk nor jerk up to make him sit, where he has only his weight with which to resist. Here, when pressure is toward the ground, the dog can brace against a force that is many times his own weight by stiffening his front legs, just as a ten-year-old boy can kneel on all fours and, with stiffened arms, easily support several hundred pounds in a gym-class pyramid.

You may be sure that the success of his rebellion will teach and condition him to resist further instruction as well as to fight corrections when, finally, he does learn the significance of the command.

From the fact that he can brace solidly with stiffened legs against the downward pull, it is evident that this pressure imposes many times more strain on the dog's anatomy than is ever applied by forward or upward force, where he can resist with no more than his own weight.

There is also more strain on the trainer. Standing balanced on one foot, the trainer is hardly in position to protect himself against a fall or a bite should a big dog use all of his resources in a violent struggle. And if he does resist, the dog could hardly be punished with a sense of fairness. After all, he was not resisting a reasonable request to do something that he understood.

Even those who most dramatically assume the foot-on-the-leash stance will quietly admit that there are some dogs on which their method doesn't work.

From the moral and mechanical truths stated above, it will be obvious that there is nothing contradictory between the advice, previously given, that it is correct to establish your authority by forcing your dog into the natural action of walking with you and the statement that you are obliged to acquaint him with the down by placing him comfortably in position until he knows what you desire him to do, without giving him the desire or the technique of bracing against it. We followed this fair procedure on the other stationary exercises, and we'll follow it on the down.

Prepare for the first lesson on the down exercise, which generally starts with the fourth week of training, by a careful study of the drawing on page 161, so that you will memorize the step-by-step procedure for properly placing your dog in the down position.

Notice how the left hand grasps the running part of the collar, the part that runs from the leash through the noose ring. If your fingers got into the noose of the collar and your dog tried to spin or whirl, your fingers could become entangled and severely injured, so keep them in the proper position.

Without hurting or choking the dog, your grip should hold the collar snugly enough to keep his neck from sliding and turning. The reason for keeping the back of your left hand up will be apparent: The left arm can be swung over the dog to bring your weight — all of it, if necessary — to bear on his back in order to push him down as you move his front feet forward from under him and place him on the down.

When you can close your eyes and visualize each step of the technique given in the illustration, you are ready to acquaint your dog with the down.

Begin by bringing the dog, at heel, from

his place of confinement and reviewing all exercises learned to date. When you reach a point where there is not the slightest contention on any exercise, make a stop and after the dog has sat automatically, give the one command — "Joe, down" — and place him in the down position exactly as shown in the illustration that you have studied.

Remember to keep the downward pressure of your left arm on the dog's back as you move his feet straight forward from under him — we want to get both ends down at once. If his legs are small enough so that you can hold them both in your right hand, there will be little chance of his outmaneuvering you with his feet; otherwise, you will have to grasp his left leg at a point high enough to prevent him from raising his right leg above the path of your arm as it moves forward to carry his feet from under him.

Do not be one of those strange individuals who try to bulldog their dog over onto his side. Nothing in the illustration is remotely similar to such an action. Again, the picture shows the collar held in the left hand, as the trainer kneels on his left knee, with the left arm bringing his weight — as much as is necessary — to bear on the dog's back, while the right hand and arm move the dog's feet forward and from under him.

Praise the dog immediately when he reaches the down position, and let him get up. As in the case of the sit, it's the down not the down-stay that we're working on.

Walk off with the dog at heel and practice the other exercises once or twice each, then repeat the placing and praising on the down.

If your dog gives you a bad time by sliding sideways out from under your arm, you can end his sliding by working with him trapped between a fence or building and yourself.

The average training period, with time spent on practicing exercises and meeting a dog's occasional challenge, will find you placing your dog on the down from ten to fifteen times, depending on whether you train for one long or two shorter periods a day.

And what if your dog isn't average but fights against your placing him down the first time?

Consider for a moment that in using our chosen technique on the down instead of the foot-on-the-leash, our first concern was with the dog's physical and mental comfort. We have attempted to introduce him to the down exercise in the fairest and most pleasant manner. As to the reasonableness of handling a dog against his protests, remember that aside from training, we are still obligated to touch and handle a dog's feet, if only to treat him for an injury or to cut his nails. Thus, even the spineless ones to whom a dog's violent, screaming protests might appear to be a real problem are left no morally correct solution other than to continue handling the dog against his wishes.

And, alas, since it is impossible to be more gentle, the troubled handler can only proceed with a deliberate fairness until the dog's rebellion against the reasonable action leaves no course but to end the dog's protests in the very definite manner prescribed in Lesson IV for dealing with the "protest biter."

Even though pussyfooting around points of contention has made the job of establishing authority much harder on both you and the dog than if you had met your obligations at the proper time, the task can still be accomplished.

For your assurance of this fact, take a look at what can be done when trainers are faced with the absolute necessity of overcoming their dog's objections to being placed on the down. There has been a rule in force in all the obedience classes that I have run that each trainer in the class will follow through on his first attempt to place his dog on the down, regardless of the animal's protest against his reasonable action. Any objecting dog is to be thoroughly convinced that he will be handled at any hour of the day or night that his master might choose. Now take a good look at the affidavit on page 17. This shows that your chances are very good. And when the dog knows that his master is going to follow through, the job is not very difficult.

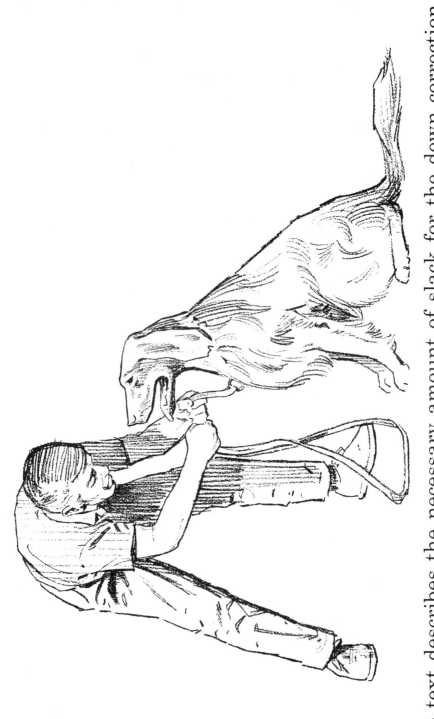

The text describes the necessary amount of slack for the down correction.

Make certain that the first correction does the job.

Sound cruel? Would it be kind to avoid trimming and shoeing the hooves of a sore-footed horse because he didn't want his feet handled?

During the training periods of the first four days spent on the down, continue to place and praise your dog in the down position. If you've done a good job of pleasantly associating the exercise with the command, your dog should be "melting" cheerfully down into position by the end of the third day's training. By the end of the fourth day's work on the exercise, you may be sure that you have given him ample time to learn the significance of your command and that, beginning with the next training period, you will be acting reasonably if you should correct him for failing to respond to the word.

To make the process of enforcing the down easy on you and your dog, drawings as well as written descriptions are provided. Study both until each step of the mechanics and the reason for it is clear in your mind.

On the fifth day, bring your dog from his place of confinement and go through the usual pattern of reviewing the exercises. After placing him on the down once or twice, make a stop and, after the dog has sat automatically, step out to where you can face him from a position that is about twenty degrees to the right of the direction in which the dog's body is heading.

With both hands grasp the leash about six inches from the collar. As a rule, this is enough slack to permit a jolting surprise on the down correction without the risk that the trainer's hands will hit the ground before his jerk can tighten the leash. For extremely short-legged breeds, such as the Dachshund, the amount of slack must be reduced accordingly.

As the drawing shows, both hands are locked tightly on the leash for maximum purchase, together with the feeling and attitude of absolute finality that is vital to an authoritative correction. Now, with the above-mentioned amount of slack hanging down in the leash, move your hands up close to the dog's neck so that your jerk will have distance to develop full momentum and explosive power before the leash can tighten and cause the dog to brace.

Next, give one — and only one — command to down: "Joe, down!"

If your dog goes down on the command, praise him warmly.

If the dog doesn't respond immediately, use your arms, shoulders, and back in a chopping stroke that jerks the leash at an angle that is down, a bit forward, and enough toward the dog's right side so that all of the force is centered on his right front leg.

Why? Simple mechanics.

Since the downward pressure prevents the

leg from moving to balance or brace, the forward pressure causes it to buckle at the joint that God put just above the dog's front foot. The dog will crumple downward and forward over his foot with very little strain on the neck.

Give him a pat to let him know that there's a pleasant reception awaiting him on the down, then let him up again. Remember — it's the down, not the down-stay, that you're working on.

The enforcement of the command was accomplished because you took the dog *off balance* with a technique based upon proper mechanics instead of trying a slow, steady, downward pull that gave him time to brace with his front legs while you bleated, "Down, down, down, now down, down" or applied insipid tugs that nagged him into greater resistance, thereby increasing the strain on his neck.

For the benefit of the more tentative members of my obedience classes, I have suggested hundreds of times that they obtain their veterinarians' opinions as to the worth of my instructions, relative to the dog's physical welfare, for correction on the down exercise. The method has received unanimous endorsement from the veterinarians they have questioned.

So, in the name of truth and simple laws of mechanics, if you should still insist on using the tugging, swinging, "bell-clapper" correction, do not call your action "kindness."

Until told differently, each time you intend to down your dog, be out in front ready to back up your command with the proper correction if your dog should be slow or uncertain in his response. Your readiness will make you an effective handler; consequently the dog will soon realize the futility of delaying his response and will be spared the large number of corrections that is the sad lot of the dog who has been nagged into resistance.

So be ready. And be just as ready to sincerely praise your dog when he goes down on a word of command. After a few days' training periods have proven that you are always ready to correct or praise, he'll probably settle for the praise.

"And," you may be asking, "what do I do if he won't down on command but drops just ahead of the correction?"

I'll tell you what you can do.

If your dog should work this "ha-ha, beat you to it" racket, make certain that you correct him more emphatically than usual.

Why?

If he has so much intelligence, initiative, and coordination that he tries to turn the exercise into a competitive game, you may be sure that he may be fairly corrected for failing to down on command. Your dog must learn that he is to down on a word of command or face the correction that will surely come, regardless of his attempt to throw you a herring by downing just ahead of your movement.

And how can he be corrected when he's lying on the ground?

Easily. Hold a six-inch length of leash in the regular manner for correction, then lift upward until the dog's neck is raised high enough to permit a regular down correction before your hand hits the ground. Don't worry that your dog will be confused by your action of pulling him up from the down position and then correcting him. Generally, with the dog that plays the game of downing just ahead of the correction, it's the trainer who is confused, not the dog.

When the dog has gone down willingly on command at least twenty-five consecutive times, you'll know that he's past the point of all-out resistance and that it's safe to risk giving a down command while you are standing upright beside your dog, just as you are when he sits automatically.

Without stooping, curtseying, or bowing, give a single command and, if the dog does not respond immediately, turn toward him, grab the leash within six inches of the snap, and drop your weight in as forceful a down-jerk as your position will permit. Once more, don't be slow or inhibited in your correction or your dog will be encouraged to resist.

Of course, as soon as he goes down on

command, he'll be getting praise instead of correction.

If he withholds response until after you've moved to correct, be certain to follow through. An obedient dog should down on a word of command without any nod or other physical cue from his master.

Few things are more pathetic than a so-called trained dog that won't down because a stiff neck or sore back prevents his master from nodding or bowing to him.

When your effectiveness as a handler has caused your dog to perform reliably under ordinary conditions, work until you get the same reliability in more distracting situations.

This second stage of reliability generally comes within three days after the first down corrections are started.

When your dog has been taken past the point of contention or argument, you can add the down exercise to your pattern of work for further practice and polishing and consider that you and your dog are ready for the next exercise.

Cadence Topsy was the first Bull Terrier to earn the titles of Champion, Utility Dog, and Tracker. She belonged to Carol Taylor of Riverside, California.

"Duke" defends his family in *The Swiss Family Robinson*. (© *Walt Disney Productions*)

Lesson IX

DOWN-STAY

You are about to start one of the most valuable exercises in basic obedience. Since it requires not the slightest physical strain, the down-stay can be used as a convenience for keeping the dog in one place for a long time. Also, because it brings no discomfort, there is nothing inhumane about increasing the dog's capacity for restraint and emotional stability by requiring him to hold the down-stay for long periods.

The down-stay differs from the sit-stay in position, but the teaching of it is much the same — only easier. Experience on the former exercise has taught your dog that "stay" means "don't move," and this combined with the fact that he already knows the down position justifies a correction if he disobeys when placed on a down and told to stay.

For your assurance of how easily and speedily your dog will learn the down-stay, I shall mention that in most obedience classes the exercise is regarded as so easily comprehended that no class time is allotted for demonstration. A handler is simply told to put his dog on the down, tell him to stay, and use a regular down correction if he gets up. Along with this brief instruction goes the usual warning against "undercorrection."

Begin the lesson with a few minutes of review on the familiar exercises. When you and your dog are performing smoothly, down him in the usual way, give a command such as "Joe, stay," and step out to face him from a location identical to that which you used for making your first down correction — no more than one step away. In fact, the corrections used when a dog breaks the down-stay are exactly the same as those used when he fails to respond to the down command.

Be sure that you step out right-foot first. (When the left foot moves first, it means "heel.") The signal you give with your left hand should be open-fingered, palm toward the dog, and as emphatic as the firm tone of your voice. Again, I am aware that the rules governing obedience trials do not permit the double command. Don't worry. Any handler capable of training a dog to stay is certainly able to limit himself to the proper command when the vividness gained by using the two in combination has caused the dog to associate each type of command with the act of staying. In the meantime, the handler, whose dog has learned that the hand motion has the same significance as the word, has a good foundation if he should ever be interested in trying the "signal exercises of advanced training."

As you stand facing the dog from a step out in front, have a few inches of slack in the leash. Previous practice in correcting the dog for failure to down on command has shown you how to get your arms and back into a correction of maximum effectiveness, so, if your dog should move from the stay, use the same technique to jerk him back to position. If he crawls toward you or in any other direction, use a jerk that sends him skidding back to the exact position where he was told to stay. It is a pitiful sight to see some dull handler pull a dog back down to position or "tow" a crawler back to a spot in the belief that this comfortable means of returning a dog will somehow accomplish the work of a correction.

And keep your mouth shut while you correct him. You told him once to down and once to stay. That's enough. If he disobeys ten times, give him ten corrections but not another command.

When your dog holds for as long as ten seconds, move back to his side by the same route you came, and let your praise tell him what a wonderful job he did. If you ask him to hold too long on his first experience with the new exercise, he'll be confused and wonder just what it is that you want.

Do not permit him to use the motion of your return nor the action of your praise as an excuse to move. Make a quick correction if he gets up before you end the exercise. When he has held a few seconds following the praise, give a heel command, start off on the left foot, and spend a minute or two on the practice of other exercises before repeating the down-stay experience.

With these short periods of reviewing familiar exercises between the repetitions of the down-stay, you will probably repeat the new exercise ten times the first day. That's enough. By the end of the day's training, he should hold for at least twenty seconds. Again, don't ask for more or settle for less.

The second day, after moving out to face your dog on the down-stay from a step out in front, you may add the distraction of a bit of motion by taking a short step to the right and then a step back to the left. If he holds the position as you take the two steps, move back to his side and praise him. If he takes your action as an invitation to a game, correct him and repeat the tempting step.

As with the sit-stay, it is fair for you to make a distracting move so long as it is not addressed directly to the dog. *To address an inviting action to the dog and then correct him when he responds would destroy confidence.*

Remember, the substance of the exercise is for your dog to remain lying in the exact spot where he was told to stay. While it is desirable that he be relaxed to the point of turning his head about or shifting his weight a bit, the turning and shifting should not move him one inch from where he was told to stay.

Don't let him get you off balance with a program of "swimlike crawling" or "progressive stretching" that takes him five or six inches from the spot where he was left. Give this kind of dog an inch and truly he will take a mile. Beware of the dog who raises up from the down-stay, then, as the handler moves to correct, drops back down, thinking to avoid correction. Obviously, since it is a stay exercise, such a dog is even more deserving of correction than if he had not returned to position — his return to position proves he knew better than to break.

In a case such as that above, where the dog toys with his mentally inferior handler, the restraint-developing values of the exercises were lost. Do not merely teach the dog the meaning of the exercises — use them to make him a better dog.

On the second day of work on the down-stay, repeat the distraction of side-stepping back and forth in front of the dog. When he is holding well, take a step farther away from him, then a step back toward him. Completion of the second day's training should find the dog holding for thirty seconds while you leave him, do the distracting steps, and return to his side.

On the third day you can enlarge the pattern of your steps until you are moving sideways and backward and forward the length of a slack leash from your dog. Lest you confuse the dog, be careful that your steps do not tighten or jerk the leash.

About this time, you may face a pitfall. There may be a temptation to try a down-stay without the leash or with your end of it lying on the ground. Keep a good grip on that leash until you are told to do differently.

From now on, return to your dog's side by circling around behind him as you did on the sit-stay. The hand should hover at a constant level over the center of the dog's back as, with full slack in the leash, you travel around close to the dog in a pattern that ends when you are in proper position to start off with the dog at heel. Only as you take one step to "break the dog loose" do you gather in the slack and rearrange the leash in your right hand. Later, when we work on another type of stay position, you will see that this technique of handling the leash on a return to the dog is not merely important, it's vital. So practice it.

By the end of the third day's training on the position, you should be able to leave your dog on the down-stay, stand facing him a slack leash length away for one minute, return, and praise him without his moving until you break him loose with the heel command.

Always be certain, when your dog breaks, to make your correction at that point where the disobedience occurs. For example, if he breaks immediately when you step out to face him, correct him from out in front and continue on with the exercise. Don't go back to his side and start the exercise all over. Likewise, if your dog turns to face you as you are moving around behind him, on your return to the heel-position snatch him back the way he came. In this "turning instance" make doubly certain that you keep your leash-jerk horizontal, not up. When he holds the position, resume your movement from the point of correction on to the completion of the exercise. Don't correct the dog and then repeat that part of the exercise which he may have done perfectly well. Make it a firm rule to always correct and continue on from the point where the disobedience occurs.

By the end of the fourth day after beginning the down-stay, your dog should hold for three minutes even though exposed to the temptations of people and animals walking nearby. Once more, do not let him consider your praise as a reason to move before you take the heel step that ends the exercise.

By now, you will find that the increasing capacity for restraint and steadiness that you are building into your dog with the down-stay will manifest itself in seemingly unrelated situations. You may notice a tendency for him to grow more resigned and relaxed, regardless of his surroundings. Later, you will learn how the stays can be used systematically to work miracles in the calming of a "geared" or restless dog. By the end of the week, the down-stay should be as familiar a part of your pattern of work as the other exercises. Your dog should now be holding for five minutes. Most important, you will be convinced that the benefits of reliability and character development obtainable from the down-stay are limited only by your own determination, constant effort, and correct technique.

Even a large dog can be lifted into a standing position.

Stay close when you begin the counterclock-wise return.

Lesson X

STAND-FOR-EXAMINATION

Unless you are above average in discernment, you might make the common mistake of thinking the **stand-for-examination** is merely a formal exercise for dog shows. The error of such thinking becomes apparent when you consider that of the 11,500 dogs referred to in the affidavit that accredits this book, approximately 15 percent were placed in training for biting problems, yet fewer than nine dogs so much as threatened the strangers who touched and examined them when they graduated from classes. Watch carefully as we work on the **stand-for-examination** and see how the exercise should be used to stop indiscriminate biting and to make a dog emotionally stable when approached by strangers.

Since there is no confusing similarity between the trainer's actions on the down-stay and the stand-for-examination, the two exercises can be conveniently started in the same period. (You will see the start of the exercise demonstrated in the illustration on page 185.)

Set the stage with the usual review of previously learned work. When your dog is performing smoothly, make a stop and acknowledge his automatic sit with a bit of praise so he'll know you like what he's been doing, and will not take your action of placing him on the stand as disapproval.

Change your grip so your right hand is holding the leash close to the dog's neck, as shown on page 185. This will keep his front end from drifting about as you work with his rear and at the same time prevent an accidental upward tug which would give the dog a cue to sit.

Next, adjust your position so that you can extend your left arm across the small of the dog's back beneath his loin, as shown in the picture.

Give a command such as "Joe, stand," then gently raise the dog to a standing position.

Remember, if you let your action or your dog's cause any upward tension on the leash as you work on the stand, your dog will think you a fool. And he'll be right. What word could better describe a person who would tell a dog to stand and, at the same time, cue him with a tug?

When he is standing, move your left hand from under him and gently stroke his side and his back in the area of his shoulders. For the time being, keep away from that area where you pushed when you taught him to sit. If the dog tries to shift from position, you can trap his movements between your arm and leg. If he sits back down, raise him up again. When he has stood for ten seconds, show your approval with praise as you heel him one step forward to where he should sit automatically. This definite ending of the exercise is to discourage the dog from ever sitting back down on the spot where he was placed on the stand. If he should try to sit before this terminating step, raise him back to a stand. If he makes 501 attempts to sit, raise him 502 times.

It is obvious that when you finish your praise and stroking, your heel command, the slackening of the leash, and the forward step must flow into one smooth operation. Certainly, it would confuse your dog if you were to stand motionless beside him while you go through the process of arranging your leash. Again, give the command, take the step, and do your leash arranging as you move.

Another method of placing the dog on the stand is to give the command, then move the leash, which is held closely and at neck level, straight forward a distance sufficient to cause the dog's front feet to adjust a couple of steps ahead as his rear end is raised to a standing position. After the praise and stroking, he is "broken loose" with a forward step, as was explained in the first example.

Because, in this second method of placing a dog, he is being stopped at the same time he is told to stand, there is a bit more possibility that he might be confused and try to sit back down. For this reason, the first procedure of standing the dog, without moving him forward, is probably better for most trainers. An exception would be the handlers of German Shepherds. Their dogs, due to singular qualities of conformation, must move their front feet forward in adjusting to their extensively angulated stance. *Whether you use the first or second method, remember two things: Never let the leash pull upward, and never let the dog sit back down until you have heeled him forward a step.*

When he has worked on the exercise about ten times each day for five days, your dog should hold a stand for half a minute as you lightly stroke his back. By now you should be ready to begin conditioning him to the approach and touch from all angles as he holds the stand, in preparation for later accustoming him to strangers.

Before we begin this conditioning process, it might be well to mention that your dog does not have to learn to stand up on command. Even in the novice obedience competition, you may place him. In fact, there is no provision made for giving him a higher score if he were to assume a standing position when he hears your command. The exercise is graded solely on what he does after he is placed in the position.

Begin the sixth day of work on the stand by placing your dog in the usual way. Let all of the leash except the grip fall from your right hand, even though it means that several feet will be lying on the ground. This is to make it impossible for you to accidentally tighten the leash as you begin to work your way around the dog.

Give a stay command and, with your left hand lightly stroking the dog near the shoulder, begin to sidestep around him in a counterclockwise pattern. Don't edge along apprehensively; move smoothly and confidently. He may be a bit distracted by your changing position and try to turn to face you or sit. Use one hand on the collar to turn him back to position and use the other hand to restand him. As you pass in front of him, you will find it convenient to change the leash grip to the left hand and do your stroking and restanding with the right. As you pass down his left side toward his rear, your unfamiliar presence at that point makes it probable that he will try to move from position. Again, one hand should go to the collar to turn him back to position and, if he should sit, the other hand should go beneath him to do the restanding. If he's a big dog, when you've worked your way around to his rear, you'll no longer be able to reach the collar, and you'll have to rely on your hands to thrust him back "the way he came" each time he turns or moves. Do not drop your grip on the leash as you use the leash hand to handle the dog. At times, you may have to move fast to head him off. After a correction, always continue your progress from where you were when the dog broke.

After you've passed behind the dog and are moving back along his right side toward the starting point, you'll find it necessary to switch the leash grip back to the right hand and do the handling with the left. When you've worked your way around the dog to the place where you started, immediately give a heel command, take a step, straighten up, and adjust to the proper leash grip — all in one motion. As you practice your exercises, periodically repeat the standing and conditioning to touch routine at least ten times each day. Three days from the time you start the circling, your dog should know the score so well that he'll stand solidly while you side-step around him an arm's length away. This will condition him to stand while you're at a distance, yet you'll be close enough to touch him occasionally and to correct.

Always move confidently while you travel around the dog, and when you're back at the starting point don't invite confusion with an interval of "squaring up" as you stand beside him, fumbling with the leash. Stop a little farther to the right than your usual heel relationship, pause for a second with the full amount of slack still hanging in the leash, then break him loose with an angling step that brings you closer together even as it ends the exercise by heeling the dog forward. Adjust to the proper leash grip after you've started the step forward — not before.

After two days of moving around your dog at an arm's length, change that circling pattern to an oval that keeps you the arm's length from his sides and rear but lets you move out to face him from a distance of three feet in front. Face him casually; don't stare at him anxiously or threateningly, as though you were about to bear down on him. If you have to move in for a correction, restand him calmly and smoothly. There are individuals whose brain waves and physical manner can prod any dog into confusion, making him take refuge in the most familiar exercise he knows — sitting.

Face the dog out in front for about five seconds, then pass the leash to the left hand, which should extend out at your side about chest level. This will enable you to hold the hand at a point directly over the middle of the dog's back. Move back toward him and continue on a casual walk that takes you past his left side, behind him, and around back to the heel position. Finish the exercise by heeling him forward one step. Remember, the only time when you are more than an arm's length from the dog is during the five seconds you pause out in front.

By staying this close as you move around him, you will have no difficulty keeping your leash hand at a constant level of your chest and centered over the dog's back even though your dog is very large. Do your praising after you finish the command with the forward step. He will know why he got the praise, even though it comes after the step. The beginning experience on the stand taught him what it is about the exercise that pleases you.

The first few periods of facing your dog from out in front will be the most difficult for both of you. After that much experience in pleasing you, he'll know that, regardless of your movements and position, he's not to move his feet.

And if he doesn't seem to know what you want and appears hopelessly confused? There are times when a dog, mired in a bog of confusion, must be taken right on through to solid ground. It is better to keep working doggedly and calmly than to follow the foolish advice of letting him rest "till his mind clears," which actually lets him sink deeper into the bog. Once more, if he sits 501 times, restand him 502 times. But remember, it is not only permissible but desirable for a dog on the stand to move his head and wag his tail in pleasure. However, he should not move his feet.

Four days after you begin to face your dog from out in front, he should be ready to be introduced to the "approach-and-touch" part of the exercise.

The person you get to do the touching can be a stranger or a friend so long as he is neither the timid, uncertain type nor a know-it-all who will disregard your careful instructions. Tell your helper to stand quietly a few feet from the dog's right side until the dog has been placed on the stand and you have taken your position out in front, as shown at right. He should then move to the dog's side casually, with what amounts to a rather indifferent attitude. Without the appearance of reaching toward him, a hand should hang impersonally near the dog's nose so that a slight move of his head will permit the dog to sniff it. When his sniff or attitude shows he's resigned to the helper's presence, the person should touch the dog confidently on the head or neck and immediately turn and walk away without the appearance of jerking back. You should then walk around the dog and break him loose in the usual way.

We want the dog to be properly approached in the beginning of this conditioning, and this "oblique approach" is the method used by experienced handlers who work with those kinds of animals that might be "spooked" if more directly addressed by word or gesture. So, in the beginning, avoid those characters who with their "way with dogs" would discourage the less receptive dogs and invite the over-friendly animals to break position. After the dog has had some successful experience on

195

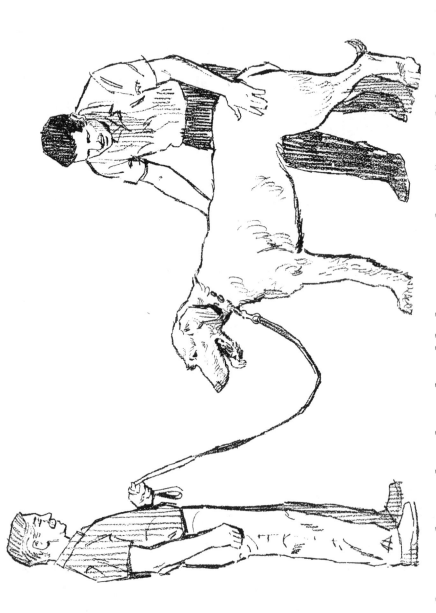

After eighteen days the dog should do a complete "stand-for-examination."

the stand, there will be time for temptations in the form of incorrect approaches.

When you are certain your helper will do as he's told, work a few of the stand-and-touch exercises into your practice pattern. Naturally, if the dog should break, from the touch or for other reasons, your job will be to move in, correct in the usual manner, repeat the part of the exercise that the dog failed, and then continue on to completion.

During the next two days, repeat the exercise exactly as started. By then your dog will be certain that he's supposed to remember your command regardless of distraction. Now that he understands fully what you want, you can generally increase the time he is left standing, and have your helper begin to touch his back (first in one place, then in another) as well as his head. At first, with this more extensive standing and touching, you'll be called upon to do a bit more correcting and re-standing; but within eighteen days of the time you begin to teach the stand for examination, your dog should hold for about one minute while you are out in front, while a stranger approaches to touch the dog's head and back and you return to complete the exercise.

Cheer up, if you've been lamenting the fact that your dog holds perfectly well on the stand until someone tries to touch him but then breaks the position. Regardless of whether he tries to play, bite, cringe, or panic, there's a solution to your problem.

The playful dog who moves to meet the one approaching him can generally be taught to think of his trainer, and where his own feet should be, by using a horizontal jerk that skids him back to where he should be restood. These forceful corrections, combined with quiet praise for a job well done, will eventually show an exuberant dog that he must still remember his responsibilities, despite the smiling eyes and friendly tail that are wonderfully appreciated. To stop such a dog from bowling over a child or precipitating other embarrassing situations is worth the hard work sometimes required.

If your dog is particularly difficult in this respect, you may have to stay close to him while your helper touches him, so that your corrections can be made faster and more effectively until your dog no longer takes your helper's approach as an invitation to a romp.

With the biter, or the shy or panicking dog who is invariably a potential biter, your responsibility to work on the stand becomes greater.

"But I don't want my dog to let people touch him. I want him to be a watchdog."

If you were about to utter the above inanity, don't. In most home situations, the indiscriminate biter is the least satisfactory watchdog because he must be closely confined and so is not ready for action in emergencies, as the properly discriminating dog would be. A ready example of how discrimination makes for the best protection dog is seen in the case of the thoroughly disciplined police-trained dog. He cannot promiscuously bite the citizens who might approach him.

There is a second fact that we must recognize: It is almost impossible to administer the all-out jerk necessary to discourage the determined biter without using a leash angle that would confuse the dog into thinking you might want him to sit. But there's an answer: Give your dog lots of preliminary experience in being approached and touched while he's on a sit-stay. Then, if he backs away or whirls to bite, you can get your back and arms into a sit-stay correction in a way that convinces him it's just not wise to move in any direction, regardless of anyone's approach. When he's had enough convincing corrections, he'll be loath to invite another by risking a bite that might pull him out of position.

Suggestions for dealing with unusually dangerous dogs are included in the chapter entitled "Problems."

Whether your dog is a biter or a "shrinker," don't kid yourself into believing you can solve the problem with the old "understanding and sweet-talk" method. Many of the misinformed have gone this syrup route only to find that their impression wasn't permanent enough to protect a person who approached their dog ill-advisedly but in friendly innocence.

You may wonder why, since he can be corrected with so much more effectiveness on a sit-stay, the stand-for-examination is ever used to condition a dog to being approached. There is a good reason. The very fact that the stand does not offer the threat of an inevitably effective correction means that it calls upon the dog to practice a greater degree of involuntary restraint. So, while the groundwork on the sit-stay may be necessary for a time, ultimately the greater good will come from being touched while on the stand. Then, too, your dog may sometime be standing or walking among a group of people when he is approached, so he should learn to control himself even though he is not influenced by the threat of a sit-stay correction. Lastly, the stand is the position in which dogs are presented for examination in the obedience and the breed rings.

Whether your dog agreed readily to the stand-for-examination or required the greater effort, within twenty-one days from starting the exercise he should hold reliably when a stranger touches him while you are standing a slack leash-length out in front.

Practice the exercise faithfully, having your helper approach the dog from all angles, touch him on the head, the back, the tail, and on the sides. You will find that the benefits of the stand-for-examination were not promised idly. There will be increased security for you, your dog will be happier and more confident, and should a veterinarian ever have to care for him, the task should be much more pleasant for the doctor and your dog.

As to indication of when you will be ready to start the next exercise, the background of experience that you and your dog have acquired through weeks of training makes it certain that you can begin another exercise seven days after the time you began instruction on the down-stay and stand-for-examination.

Obedience training has become popular in Mexico. American and Mexican Ch. Merrywood's Candy of Pintura, American U.D. and Mexican P.U., was the first Shetland Sheepdog to achieve all these titles. Candy was owned by the Lydon Lippincotts of San Bernardino, California.

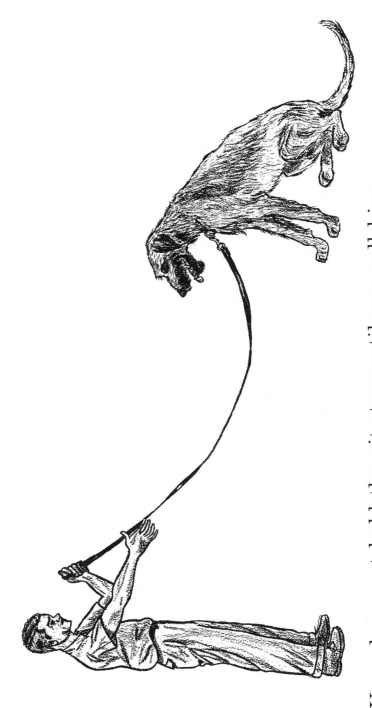

Your dog must hold the sit-stay until you call him.

Lesson XI

RECALL

If you were to walk through a residential district and ask the first ten dog owners you chanced to meet how they would feel about turning their dogs loose in an unfenced area where there was danger or great distraction, you would find few who would be willing, and the rest would regard your question as ridiculous. You would get all kinds of reasons for declining your proposition. You might learn of ordinances against having a dog off-leash, find that some "love their dogs too much" to risk their being unrestrained, and be informed that some dogs have always been confined and there is no intention to ever risk the chance of a runaway.

On the surface, the above, like many similar lines of reasoning, does sound creditable. Lots of cities do have leash-laws — and with justification. It would be cruel to free an uncontrollable dog in a dangerous situation. But these facts don't make a point, they point to a weakness. Doors and gates are left open. Dogs do get out. Emergencies do occur — often to the injury of the dog or the embarrassment of his master. Then, too, it is a sad thing for a dog, when a vacation takes his family to the outdoors, to have to remain on leash because he might "run away" or meddle in the affairs of others. Such a dog is generally deprived for life from sharing the freedom of new places with his master, who might have been "too kindly" to earn the dog's respect.

However, regardless of how restrained the life a dog might be forced to live, there is still a reason, or rather an absolute obligation, to teach a dog to come unfailingly when called. It is the obvious fact that there never can be full understanding between a master and a dog he cannot control.

So, you may ask, with safety, convenience, and understanding all demanding that a dog come when he is called, why is it that so few owners teach dogs obedience to the command?

These individuals, who are unable to teach their dogs to come when they are called, can be divided into three general classifications: the lazy handlers who won't make the effort, the misinformed, and the pigheaded persons. Typical of the third classification is the person whose thoughts are so occupied with trying to describe what he thinks is an unusual or exceptionally difficult problem that his mind is a solid wall of obsession that no ray of enlightenment can penetrate.

If you are not lazy and will keep your mouth closed and your mind open, I can provide you with a method of teaching the recall that will eventually result in a reliability of performance which will amaze you.

Though the goal of the recall exercise is to be able to control the dog off-leash, it is vital to work toward that goal a single step at a time, even when some of those steps seem unrelated to controlling the dog at liberty. The first of these steps is a groundwork of experience where it is mechanically impossible for the dog to fail to respond to the recall. This is another way of saying that he must always be on leash when he is called, until that specific time when you will be told to remove the leash. Until then, by confinement or other measures, avoid those booby traps where you demonstrate your ineffectiveness by calling the dog when you cannot make him come back. This job of avoiding difficult situations until you are prepared to cope with them may take some planning, but it will make your job easier.

Let's get started on that groundwork of experience. For a few minutes, review all exercises previously learned. Now comes our first problem. Not with the dog — with you. You'll probably want to explain that your dog knows enough to always come perfectly when on leash; it's off-leash that he doesn't obey. That's fine. Let's just continue to have him "come perfectly" a few hundred times while he's on the leash. Or perhaps you will argue that there's no connection between the precision of a dog sitting in front of you and reliability

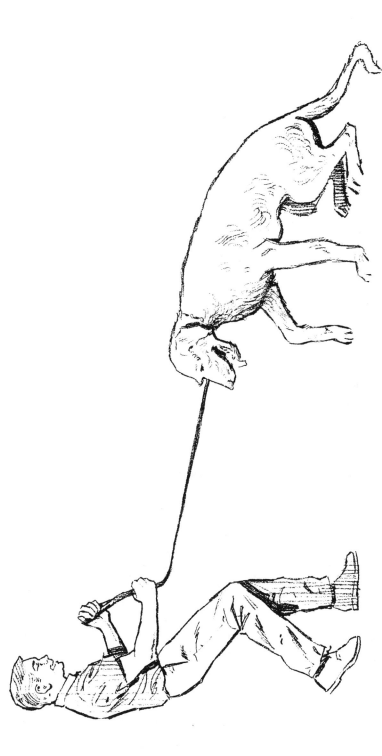

Your dog must hold the sit-stay until you call him and bring him in, hand over hand.

Bring him in, hand over hand, to a sitting position in front of you.

of performance. There is a connection, and before we're finished, you will see it. A dog, like a man, rarely gives more than you ask of him. The dog that's asked to do something as sloppy and indefinite as merely coming back to his master soon will lapse into a pattern where he comes back to a point just out of the handler's reach.

After throwing his master the "herring" with a few of these token recalls, the dog will probably make a game of dancing about just a bit farther away. This is especially probable if his competitive spirit has been kindled by having his handler make a few lunges at him. Now you know why we're going to ask more than for the dog to merely come back near his master. We're going to teach him that "come" means all the way back to a definite sitting position in front of the handler.

Even then, the exercise won't be finished, nor is the dog to relax his attention toward his master. He must be alert for the command that tells him to do the "finish," at which time he'll be required to move to the heel position and there to await either a final command or a release.

Always bear in mind that this formal recall is not window dressing nor eyewash but a procedure that requires so much of the dog that should he, manlike, give less than his best, he is still so occupied with doing a specific thing perfectly that his "less than best" brings him close to the proper position.

Further, by having to concentrate on executing perfectly the finish of the exercise, which ends only when he has moved around to his master's side, he is not given opportunity for the mental lapse and consequent unreliability, as is the case when he is asked to perform a casual recall which does not demand his full concentration.

Now back to laying that "good foundation" for the later, off-leash enforcement. Leave your dog on a sit-stay and face him from a slack leash length away. As you may notice in the illustration on page 203, the hand loop of the leash is held in the left hand. This is because most handlers can more efficiently reach out to grip and reel the slack with the right hand, and as you have learned by now, indefinite, fumbling movements do not give the dog a sharp picture of what you want.

Don't do any clasping and reeling until the dog has held his sit-stay for at least half a minute. The mistake of bringing him to you immediately would cause him to take your action of facing him as an invitation to break the stay and come to you. After he has resigned himself to waiting for the required time, give a recall command — "Joe, come" — then instantly reach out and reel the leash, hand over hand, until his head is directly in front of you and approximately a foot and a half distant.

Though you move swiftly to let him know that he should not delay in starting or coming, your actions must have the smooth clarity of instruction, not the sharpness of a correction.

When your dog has reached the proper spot in front of you, give a command to sit and, if he fails to do so, give a light, upward correction — light because this may be the first time he has been asked to sit facing his master, and honest confusion must not be treated as disobedience.

The moment he's seated squarely in front of you, reach over and praise him. Then give a heel command as you make a right-about turn and adjust the leash in a manner that brings the dog into the proper position for walking. Spend some time where you think it is most needed on the practice of other exercises, and then repeat the instruction on the recall.

Don't permit the dog to take your act of stepping out and facing him as a cue to break the sit-stay and come to you. It is disobedience, not obedience, if he comes to you before he is called, and he should get the usual correction for breaking the sit-stay. *The probability of his anticipating and "jumping the gun" will be lessened if you will vary the time he has to wait for the command, thus showing him the exercise is not a rhythmic routine of staying and coming.*

Guard against becoming one of those compromising characters that blurts "Come" as he sees the dog about to start, thinking that this changes the dog's disobedience to obedience. Such a person is fooling himself, not the dog. Now and then you'll get a bad break when the dog starts before the command is completely spoken but is too far completed for you to withhold. In these rare instances, you can only follow through and bring him on in to a sitting position in front of you. This "coinciding" of the command and the dog's anticipation will occur less often as your dog gains experience in holding for the varying periods. In a later lesson, we'll discuss measures of correcting this "trigger-happiness" when the dog is sufficiently seasoned to permit their reasonable use.

It is important to the growth of his reliability, and to the preparation for the finish part of the exercise, that your dog sit accurately in front of you. If he persists in sitting out of position, you may be required to lean out swiftly and guide him into position with either your right or left hand as the leash enforces the sit. At first, the hand in his side is just a gentle instruction, but if his inaccuracy continues, let its speed increase until it becomes a sharp chop that reminds him he'll be much more comfortable if he concentrates on sitting properly.

Control on the stay, certainty of response, and accuracy on the sit are three reasons you should continue practicing the exercise on leash even though it means reeling fast to keep ahead of a dog that seems to have learned the exercise perfectly.

On the average, a handler will practice the recall ten times each day. By the end of the third day, your dog should be so responsive to the pattern of "stay," "come," and "sit" that you will feel prepared to begin the "finish," which is that part of the exercise where the dog moves from his position in front of you around behind you to complete the exercise at your left side.

Walter Pidgeon and Gilles Payant chat on their way back from a fishing trip. (From *Big Red*, © *Walt Disney Productions*)

From this position your leg thrust would
have enough power to move an automobile.

Lesson XII

FINISH

You may be surprised to find that your dog has already made considerable progress in learning the finish.

"How could he have learned what I haven't taught him?" you ask.

You've done some teaching when you didn't realize it. You can prove this with a simple experiment. First, let's take another look at the specific action of the finish. It is that pattern where the dog, after coming and sitting in front of the handler, takes a command to travel clockwise around behind the handler until he is able to sit in the correct heel position at the handler's left side.

Back to that experiment. Place your dog on a sit-stay and call him in the usual way. After he has sat in front of you for a few seconds, instead of turning right-about and walking off with the dog as you formerly did, give a heel command, and, without any hesitation, walk backward four or five steps. Then stop just as confidently as you do when walking forward. When you walked in reverse, your right side actually became the "heeling side" in the mind of the dog, and he walked and sat automatically at that side just as he does at your left when you're walking forward.

Give the command "Heel" and take a backward step.

Let's carry the experiment a bit further. Leave him and call him again. As before, after he has sat properly, give him a heel command and walk backward. Then, without a halt, pass the leash behind your back, and take a few steps ahead, shifting to the correct leash grip as you do so. You'll find that as you changed the direction of your walking from backward to forward, your dog, working to keep you on his own right side, moved around behind you to your left. Remember, to the dog your correct heeling side is that which is to the right of him when he is walking. That's why, when you change from walking backward to forward, he adjusts by crossing behind to keep you on his right. Again, when you stop, he sits automatically.

Your dog's response to your actions will show that you achieved more than you realized during the time you taught him to heel and sit automatically. It was your principle of demanding attentiveness and instant response that will make the movements of the finish seem logical to the dog and the teaching quite easy — logical because the finish will be addressed to the dog in a manner based on the heel and sit, two exercises with which the dog is already familiar, and quite easy because you will use leverage to lessen the physical task if your dog should offer resistance.

When the time comes that your dog has

Pass the leash around behind you and step forward.

learned the finish, he should perform the exercise on a command, without any movement from you. Consequently, the logic of our "walking and stepping approach" must progress to a point where we can pass the initiative and responsibility for acting on command to the dog.

To most fully appreciate the physical help you'll get from the correct technique that we'll use for instruction, try this procedure. Park a car in neutral, with the brake off. Hook your leash to the bumper or bumper guard. Stand facing the car two feet back from where the leash is attached. Have just enough slack in the leash to permit the hand holding it to be firmly locked behind your right leg.

I repeat "behind your right leg" because experience has shown me that a large number of handlers become very confused as to right and left, to say nothing of the exact position of the hand.

Step back with a bend in your right leg and dig your toe into the ground. This action will take the slack out of the leash but not pull. Now straighten the right leg and rock yourself backward with a push of the left leg. It may be that the leverage of your body against the fulcrum of the low-held leash actually moved the car a few inches.

It should occur to you that the drag of the car is heavier than that of a dog — even the biggest dog.

If the dog fails to sit automatically as forward motion ceases, give the usual sit correction.

Now try the wrong technique, with your arm extended out from your body, in the manner in which unthinking handlers will often try to move a big dog. The arm of a powerful man, when extended out from the body, can be restrained by the single finger of a person with much less strength. From the foregoing, you will see the stupidity of trying to move the dog around with a backstroke of your extended arm.

Now let's apply our technique of logic and leverage to the dog.

Do the recall from the sit-stay in the usual way, and after the dog has come and sat in front of you, wait a few seconds, then arrange the leash hand behind your leg exactly the same as when you pulled against the car.

Give an emphatic command such as "Joe, heel" and take a single step backward as you did against the car, but, as the step moves the dog from his position to a point at your right side, pass the leash behind you to your left hand. Without stopping or slowing your movement, reach across your body with the right hand and add its grip to that of the left as you take a single, strong step forward that encourages the dog to heel around behind you to the correct spot at your left side. The accompanying illustrations demonstrate this correct technique. If the dog fails to sit automatically as forward motion ceases, make the usual sit correction.

Study the drawings carefully and work to get a rhythmic effectiveness into the pattern of stepping back, passing the leash behind you, and stepping ahead. Practicing the leash handling and stepping routine without the dog will sometimes smooth out your actions so that you can handle him more smoothly. When properly executed, the completion of the backward step and forward step should place you in the same location as when you started the exercise, except that now the dog is sitting in the heel position at your left side. A bit of practice will enable you to apply the technique efficiently.

Here are solutions to some of the minor problems that might arise.

If there seems to be a confusion — real or phony — that causes your dog to delay in his start or to sit down before he gets completely around to the left side, there is a trick you can use to set him right. About one out of three times, as you do the finish, instead of following the back step with a single step forward, follow it with several running steps forward before you stop. If your dog delays his start, because he felt you "really weren't going anyplace," this will convince him that he'd better get started for that "heel side." And if he should attempt to lag or sit before he gets around to your left, your momentum plowing into the leash will show him that your heel command might mean that you're going farther than one step, and he'll be much more comfortable if he gets clear around to where he's ready to go with you.

If he fails to sit when he gets around to that "safe spot," correct him; however, don't worry about a crooked sit or a position that's a bit far ahead or behind. Just see that he gets completely around and sits and that you show your appreciation when he does. Ways of tidying up his performance will be dealt with in the lesson on polishing.

The average trainer will repeat the recall and finish instructions about ten times a day. After seven days of work on the recall, the last four of which included the finish, you may feel that the period of instruction has been completed and the period of correction may be fairly begun.

Henceforth, while practicing the fundamentals of the recall, call the dog from the sit-stay as usual, but instead of reeling the leash to prevent his delay in starting or coming, give him a full second to make his own decision. Then, should there be a lag in his response, correct him with a stiff, two-handed jerk that propels him all the way to the proper position in front of you.

If this "propelling" is the immediate and inevitable result of each failure to respond, failures will soon be eliminated. Do not make the attention-dulling mistake of repeating a command or reminding him of your existence with little tugs. Give one command and see that he obeys it.

Let your praise for a good performance be just as emphatic as your corrections. It's the emphasis on each that makes the contrast between the two.

At the same time you begin correcting for disobedience on the foregoing part of the recall, you can begin to enforce the finish part of the exercise. Why you may reasonably do this after only four days of instruction, as against seven on the first part, is at once apparent when you remember that in comprehending the finish, your dog was merely required to perform the familiar exercises of heeling and sitting in a pattern your instructive steps showed. Four days is ample time for him to learn the meaning of your command and to justify your correction if he does not respond to the single word.

As always, preparedness is the key to an effective correction.

The illustration on page 214 shows a dog that has been called to a sit position in front of his handler. Notice that the hand is locked securely, well around behind the leg. Now, however, allow a sag of six inches of slack to fall into the leash, instead of having it taut as shown in the illustration of the back steps being used for instruction. More than six inches of slack would cause the corrective action to be expended without its full effect reaching the dog; a lesser amount would not permit the momentum of the correction to build up into an authoritative jolt.

When your leash has this proper amount of slack, give a single command for the dog to heel. If he takes the initiative and responds promptly and without further cue, praise him when he gets around to your left side. If he does not respond immediately, thrust your right leg backward in a step that jerks the leash in an effective correction and starts the dog on his path around behind you. Pass the leash behind you to the left hand as you take the forward step back to position; then you will be prepared to take a few running steps if he tries to sit down before he gets around you.

The fast, jolting step backward will show him that he can't beat the correction once it starts, and the only way to avoid discomfort is to respond the moment he hears the command. The occasional practice of taking a few running steps forward will deter him from the "out-of-sight, out-of-harm" maneuver of sitting down before he gets around to the proper spot.

Sometimes it takes many corrections to convince a dog that it's better to start promptly than to risk a correction that he cannot outmaneuver. On this particular exercise, there is a great danger of a trainer spoiling his dog's progress by withholding correction because ten or twelve efforts have failed to influence the dog.

If you have done an average job of working on the four days of "instructive steps," your dog should be walking freely through the pattern of the finish, which is evidence that he knows what you want. This being the case, do not relent if ten corrections in a row get you nothing but shrieks of protest from the dog and castigations from spectators who would brand you "beast."

Determination and the proper technique will make it certain that your dog will be doing the recall and finish reliably and smoothly within four days after starting the corrections. In fact, he may be working so smoothly that you might be tempted to try a little work off-leash. Don't do it. Don't gamble. One loss is sure to cancel out any number of wins. You'll proceed much easier and faster toward your goal of off-leash control if you will concentrate on perfecting each exercise on leash. When the time comes, we'll start the off-leash work the right way, which means without a gamble.

There — you've started the last of those exercises commonly summed up as "novice obedience." You've learned that demanding response to a command does more than merely control a dog on a leash. Practice of the exercises has developed your dog's sense of responsibility and increased his emotional stability. Magically, it seems, his confidence, reliability, and happiness have increased. This is natural. As his performance improves, he gets more and more of your praise.

Keep this fact in mind as we begin the next lesson, which will be devoted entirely to practicing and polishing the exercises your dog has learned, so that you might be prepared to get the fullest benefits when the time comes to start work on the off-leash control.

Until now, that piece of equipment called a tab has remained unused. You may have wondered just why you have it. But you'll come to agree that it's one of the handiest articles you own. In order to use it most effectively, you must familiarize the dog with the feel of the tab hanging on his collar. For the rest of your training program, see that it's attached to the dog's collar, as shown, for two hours of his leisure time each day. Make sure, if you have a shortlegged dog, that the tab is not so long as to catch his feet, but don't concern yourself if it swings against his legs.

Attitude

Often, when one is engaged in training a dog, the importance of the trainer's attitude is largely neglected. The scientist to which the affidavit of this book refers presented facts to a large convention of experienced trainers on the harmful effects of indeterminate handling. Many in his audience were qualified class instructors who had witnessed how a questioning, probing attitude in handlers could nag a dog into neurosis. This not only refers to tentative, watered-down physical corrections but to the effect of the handler's brain waves, which a dog can sense so effectively. This receptivity to electrical manifestations of brain waves also debunks the theory of a threatening dog smelling a person's fear-scent even when the frightened human is downwind from the dog.

That a dog is strongly influenced by the attitude of a person who gives him a command is well known to experienced trainers. When such a trainer prepares to demonstrate a correction with a dog that has been taught an excercise by a person who failed to give an effective correction, and food rewards had no effect, such a dog will often cue instantly from the instructor's positive attitude. This has happened even after the dog failed to respond to commands from the handler who actually taught him the exercise but never established authority.

Some individuals are distressed even by the thought of making an about-turn, so the dog is surprised by the self-inflicted jerk of the long line. Doubtlessly, such a person would be equally distressed and commiserative if his dog ran head-on into a tree and yelped in pain at the impact.

When an instructor prepares to demonstrate the right attitude to such a person, he asks if the dog understands the exercise. When assured that the dog understands what is wanted of him, something takes place in the instructor's mind. He blocks out any consideration of failure to make the dog obey his command. The only picture in his mind is that of the dog performing in response to the command and being physically set to meet any hesitation with a correction.

But you feel you lack the attitude or finality that is part of making a good correction and wonder if anything can be done to compensate for your weakness. Yes, there is a formula that can help you stiffen your spine and be more commanding and less entreating. When you teach a new exercise, extend the placing or mechanical conditioning of the dog to where all resistance to being manipulated has disappeared. This lack of resistance will show you the dog knows what is wanted and will assure you of the fairness of correcting if your command is not obeyed.

Be certain to praise emphatically when the dog cooperates with your efforts.

Children are proud to win in "Novice Y" competition, which features the on-leash exercises. Here is Raymond Koehler, son of the author, with his first trophy. *(Photo by Henry C. Schley)*

Lesson XIII

POLISHING

Up to now, your dog has learned seven exercises. Through the practice of them, he has become a bit more easily managed on leash and is somewhat improved in general conduct. This happened within eight weeks of training. If you are thorough in your efforts, your dog will gain more in obedience and character within the next seven days than he has to date. More, you'll both be ready to start the fundamentals of off-leash control. This degree of "readiness" must never be guessed at. That's why you'll have need of an unusual bit of equipment — a piece of common store string about a foot long. Nothing stronger will do.

HEELING AND SITTING

Because the heeling and sitting exercises are nearly always practiced and used together, the techniques of polishing them will be dealt with in a single section. Before you begin, turn back to page 79 and check the leash grip and manner of starting. It may be that you've developed a bad habit or two, which review will help you correct.

When ready, bring your dog from his place

of confinement and lay out a pattern of distracting points, such as you have been using in conjunction with your right-about turns. Don't use the same ones. This is to be a test of response in strange situations. If your training area permits, use at least three temptations and be certain that they are as appealing as those you have been using. Here are a few examples to add to those that might have occurred to you: another dog, possibly one in training, so that each could serve as a distraction for the other; the open door of your automobile, which will show you whether you have brought him to a state where he would decline a stranger's invitation to jump into a car; or people in unusual positions and engaged in unusual activities, such as playing games.

When your distractions are arranged, bring your dog into the area at heel and start using them in the usual way, making momentum-packed right-abouts at the instant the dog indicates that his attention has been drawn from you. Because of previous experience, he'll soon be showing a strong disinterest in all of the temptations. At this point, you can alternate your right-abouts with left turns. Here's how you can do so most effectively: Move toward a distraction in an extremely fast walk or a trot. As you draw near it, slow down and make a left turn. If the dog's interest had left you, he was unaware of your action and was made quite uncomfortable by your left knee. The big difference between your present use of these turns and your early practice is one of degree. Now, when your dog apparently cannot be distracted, the pattern of temptations you'll use during your week of "polishing" will give him hundreds of opportunities for doing the "right thing." This means hundreds of opportunities to strengthen his character by resisting temptation. And you'll have hundreds of opportunities to show him that, when temptation is resisted and he turns his mind to you, the result is praise.

Each day, during the week of polishing, you should work to increase the strength of distractions just as consistently as a guide-dog trainer works to assure that the temptations he supplies in training are stronger and more unusual than any of those which his dogs meet when they are guiding the blind on dangerous streets.

In addition to the technique of using temptations and turns, there is something you can do to increase your dog's attentiveness and, in addition, assure that he will heel in the proper position. Twenty seconds' use will convince you of its effectiveness. If you are skeptical, have someone time your actions and see.

Walk along with your dog at heel and turn, as if for the usual right-about. But now as you pivot, take three running steps, then slow to your normal walking gait and continue on your way. There was no slack-off of the leash, so if your speed at the time of the turn was doubled, your dog had half of the usual time in which to change direction and avoid a jerk. Do not confuse this "jerk," which is the natural result of your suddenly increased speed, with an argumentative "arm jerk." The first supplies the dog with a reason for increasing his speed. The second supplies confusion.

Make three of these turn-and-speed-up maneuvers, then make a turn at your normal walking speed. Amazed? It appears your dog might be pulled by a magnet, so increased is his attentiveness and the speed with which he reverses direction. But he wasn't pulled by anything. Certainly not the leash. He has simply learned that your turn might be followed by increased speed and was headed in the right direction long before the leash tightened. As your "timer" will verify, the time on the actual turns and running steps amounted to less than twenty seconds.

For the rest of the week let all of your right-abouts, and right turns as well, be of this speeded-up variety. With the right turn, as with the "about," the speed-up is made just as direction is changed. Practice making some turns without a dog, handling your feet in the manner shown in the foregoing pictures until you have a feeling of well-balanced emphasis. If you do your part, the dog will turn good "square" corners and heel attentively in the correct position.

AUTOMATIC SIT

The automatic sit, used in the pattern of distractions along with the about-turns, will make another contribution to your dog's character. Intersperse your turns with stops, particularly at those points where the dog seems a bit inattentive. If he fails to sit immediately, correct him so that he'll be reminded to always take distraction as a cue to think of you.

If your dog is one that sits out of position, approach the problem by admitting the truth. If he is heeling in a correct position and sits instantly when you stop, it stands to reason he will be sitting in proper relation to you. If he is heeling improperly, there is small reason to think he will sit properly. Further, if he is heeling correctly but you make the mistake of giving him time to take a step or two after you stop, he is certain to move ahead. No more can be, nor need be, said on this fact. Possibly your dog might heel and sit correctly but then "scootch" ahead or around in front so that he can look at you. "Unscootch" him with a jerk that brings him, airborne, back to where he knows he should be sitting.

"Scootching" backward can generally be corrected by reducing the leash-slack just as you stop, so that the dog can't back up without tightening the collar on himself. Of course, if he's a wise guy that defiantly moves back, even though he knows the right spot is beside you, you might have to "unscootch" him with a stiff jerk that brings him back into the proper position.

Alignment, because of the way the dog is facing, is a bit more difficult to correct. Speedy success depends on how well you follow instructions. If your dog regularly swings his rear away from you and faces you as he sits, bring the side of your stiffened left hand down in a sharp chop that would be certain to catch your dog in the loin if he were following his usual habit of swinging his rear away from you. If the rear were not swinging away, the loin would not get out where the descending hand would hit it. Instead, the hand could be used to give him a pat in appreciation of his good performance.

Do not make yourself ridiculous by working to push or hammer the dog into position after he has sat. Catch him on the way down. Three or four experiences will reveal that your dog is becoming aware that the hand is ready to meet any "sidewinding." And you'll be quite impressed by his efforts to keep himself in line.

If those efforts should cause him to turn too far the other way, you'll face a problem common to all who train animals: that of counter-correcting when a correction has influenced the student past the desired point. If so, counter-correct with a leash jerk, so that he's turned back into proper alignment.

Whether you are using your hand to catch his loin, or a leash jerk in the other direction, your dog must never feel you are exasperated or angry when you make the correction. So keep your action mechanical, not emotional.

There is a never-fail way to discourage a dog from "scootching" around in front of you. Stop and give him plenty of opportunity to get all the way around and into your path. Give a heel command and start out with the biggest, most powerful step you can muster — straight ahead. Feel no compunctions if a big dog receives a solid thump or a smaller one is knocked out of the way. There is plenty of room at your side, and it was the dog's foolish decision to move into your path, so don't cheat him of the consequences of his mistake. Don't be a spaghetti-spined handler who stupidly detours when his path is blocked.

Herbert Spencer said: "The ultimate effect of shielding men from the effects of folly is to fill the world with fools." The same truth applies to the world of dogs. Let your dog learn.

THE DOWN

Just as is true of all other exercises, the

benefits to the dog's character are greatest when he is required to down promptly when subjected to distraction. If a particular kind of temptation, at first, seemed to make your dog inattentive when heeling or sitting, follow through by requiring him to down in those same distracting situations.

You may also find it necessary to do a bit of work on the down position — your position first, the dog's second. If you have continued to stoop, gesture, or curtsey when giving a down command, stop that bad habit during the week of polishing. Really, you might sometime want him to down when your back is too sore to bend. Show your dog that, if he waits for a movement from you when he's told to down, he's waited too long, for your only move will be to correct. And, if he tries to "beat the correction," snug up the leash until it is taut and give a hard jerk down regardless of how flat and apologetic his belated down places him. Your dog will be likely to down accurately if he downs promptly. If he should twist or "swim" from position, after he has gone down, move him back with a snatch or jerk on the leash. Don't use a pull.

The technique of giving a heel command and plowing straight ahead, as you did on the sit, will show your dog that he'll be uncomfortable if he allows his down position to slop over into your path.

Often, when speed and accuracy on the down

are being emphasized, a dog will anticipate a command and immediately after sitting will drop in what amounts to an "automatic down." Though this is undesirable, your dog is actually attempting to please you, and with cold mechanics and in such a way that he'll not feel you are unappreciative of his efforts, you must arrange for him to break himself of the fault. Provide enough slack for him to start down, but not enough for him to get there. Unconcernedly, let him run out of slack a few times, and he'll start to wait for the command before downing.

SIT-STAY AND DOWN-STAY

Because the same principles of polishing apply to the sit-stay as to the down-stay, we can deal with both exercises in this one section. At this point in his training, to have your dog do a sit-stay and then follow immediately with a down-stay can cause confusion. Often a dog will break the sit-stay by lying down or break the down-stay by sitting up. Corrections for such disobedience will be much less apt to confuse your dog if, after you finish one of the exercises, there is an interval of work on other things before you practice the second stay position. So, by time intervals, or by interspersing other exercises, keep the stays separated until the exactness of each is clearly in the dog's mind.

You may find when you start polishing the dog's stay positions that previous experience with your pattern of distractions has made him quite suspicious of temptations and that he seems very willing to keep his attention on you and the job at hand. By the end of the first day's work in that pattern, he should be holding a sit-stay for two minutes and a down-stay for five minutes, while you face him from a leash length away and then return by circling around behind him to his right side in order to finish the exercise by breaking him loose with a heel step.

From this point on, you'll gain reliability by having your dog do his stays in proximity to new distractions. By now you have doubtless become quite expert in obtaining strange people and animals to walk and run near your dog, so we will leave the procurement of the distractions to your own ingenuity.

Perhaps you would like to know the point of distraction beyond which even the best training and conditioning cannot assure a dog's reliable performance. The point might be said to coincide with that where the "instinct for self-preservation" would logically take over. Certainly, it would be unfair to ask a dog to hold when it appeared that he was going to be struck or attacked. However, don't let your dog bamboozle you with a lot of phony fears. Noises of cars backfiring and traffic roaring, such as a guide-dog constantly experiences, are not reasons for disobedience or panic. Nor is the fact that another animal is running in close proximity justification for your dog to move from a stay. Licensed judges do not regard a dog running wildly about a ring as a reason for dogs doing stays in that ring to break their positions.

Here is a bit of magic you can use, along with your distractions, to make your dog wonderfully solid on his stays. Select a building with both angles of the corner unobstructed for at least ten feet (bushes or other objects might entangle your leash or hamper your handling). Place your dog on a stay about two and a half feet back from the end of the building. Then step around the corner so you are standing a loose leash length from the dog and hidden from his sight.

From the dog's standpoint, you have now disappeared. Chances are he'll break. If he comes toward you, you'll see him. If he goes away, the leash will tighten. In either case, you will be informed of his break and can move to correct him. Since he cannot see through the building, he won't know how far away you are, but experience will show him that you certainly can get to him in a hurry.

Unfortunately, the leash movement will not inform you if the dog should go down from a sit-stay or sit up from a down-stay. If your dog should give you trouble in this way, your chance to make the necessary correction will depend on having a properly placed mirror to let you see his actions or having someone to watch and signal you.

Gradually increase the length of these corner stays until, by the end of the week, your dog will hold the two minutes on the sit-stay and the five minutes on the down-stay with you hidden from his sight.

There is another effective way to make your dog more reliable on his stays. This is especially useful in dealing with the dog that tries to run away or in other ways dodges correction.

After the end of your longe line has been tied to a post or tree, the dog is brought to the area and placed on one of the stays about three feet from where the line is tied. After the snap has been fastened to the collar, the leash is removed, and the handler gives a stay command and walks away. Though tied, the fifteen-foot line provides so much slack that there is no feeling of physical restraint.

Actually, in even the most limited direction, the dog could run twelve feet. But if he did break, there would be no opportunity to avoid correction by running. The line would bring him up short and hold him, even though the handler was returning from a great distance. The more you use this facility, the more you will understand that your dog is being restrained, not physically but by his recognition of the inevitability of correction. Progressively increase the distance and time you are away from your dog, and you'll see immense growth in his capacity for restraint on both stay positions.

As always, insist that your dog hold until you have finished the exercise in the proper manner. It's his turn then: Show him with sincere praise that you understand what a wonderful guy he really is.

RECALL

You can forget the use of distractions while polishing the recall. As you will see — and you certainly will see — your dog will lose his interest in distractions in a matter of seconds after using the implement described in the next lesson. Now we're concerned solely with obtaining the utmost in accuracy, so that after his "conversion" assures response on leash or off, you may be certain that he'll respond accurately, too.

This working for accuracy means that you'll have to be very consistent in the use of your leash and hands. Each time your dog sits (after *recalling*) too far away from you, snub him closer with your leash. As mentioned earlier, a good distance is so that his head is about a foot and a half in front of you. You should be ready to lean forward and, with your most convenient hand, cut off any attempts to sit to one side or sideways. Previous experience on this correction should have made you quite expert at getting enough force into these "side chops" to make the dog aim for the comfort and praise that awaits him in a position directly in front of you.

FINISH

The corrections explained in the lesson teaching the recall and finish should be used, when needed, to encourage a prompt and accurate finish. In addition to the jolting back-step (used when a dog is slow to begin the finish), and the gimmick of breaking into a run to correct the dog that stops half-way around you can now use your practiced hand to straighten up his final sit position at your left side. As on the recall, those hand movements should progress from the first gentle reminders to the final, sharper encouragement.

STAND-FOR-EXAMINATION

While polishing the stand-for-examination, no distractions should be used that will turn the dog's attention from the person who approaches and touches him. The more fully conscious the dog is of that person's actions, the more the purpose of the exercise is fulfilled. The actions should now be varied somewhat in manner and extent.

Having had considerable practice in holding the stand with you out in front, and while your helper approaches from a few steps away, your dog should now hold while the approach is made from as much as fifty feet away. From this distance your helper comes to the dog more as a stranger would approach, which would not be true if the dog had been eyeing him from a short distance away. Since the approach takes longer, the dog gets practice in holding for a greater period.

You can see the importance of having your helper vary the direction of his approaches — strangers, who blunder up to gush over your dog, do so from all directions. They will also come toward him at varying speeds, so have your helper move both slowly and rapidly, but never threateningly.

Another change: The dog may now be "gone over" more thoroughly, being required to hold while he is touched on the head, shoulder, back, and under the chest.

Here is a very useful procedure, especially if you should want to exhibit your dog in the obedience or breed rings. Have your helper push down, but without authority, in the region of the dog's hips, just hard enough so that the dog must tighten his muscles and resist a bit, but not so hard that the resistance will be overridden. As the dog's resistance to the hand is felt, the person should smoothly turn and leave the dog; you should return in the usual way and praise him. By very gradually increasing the hand pressure in a way to encourage resistance, your dog will be brought to understand that you are very pleased with the way he "pushes back up" and in other ways works to resist pressures that might move him from the stand position.

Want to prove this to yourself? Watch the utility exercises in the obedience ring and see the trained dogs in this class as they stand, off leash, minute after minute, while part of the time a strange man examines them. Compare this demonstration of control and concentration, achieved through training, with the manner in which the handlers of dogs in the conformation classes of the breed-ring must finagle and fuss to keep their dogs standing in one place when the judge wants to examine them.

Any disobedience on the stand should be met with the corrections given in the lesson devoted to that exercise but met a little more forcefully. By now your dog should have enough experience on the stand so that a hand raising him "sharply" will convince, not confuse. Notice I said "a hand," not the leash. He will still be confused by any upward tug on the leash.

The piece of string, described at the start of this lesson, will show you how well you have done the week's work of polishing. It will also show you some very interesting things about yourself and your dog.

The ends of the string are tied together, the loop put through the collar ring, and then passed back through itself to form a second, six-inch loop to which your leash can be snapped. If a chain is "no stronger than its weakest link," your leash and collar unit is not stronger than the string that joins it. That's the way we want it.

Start your first training period, *after your week of "polishing" has been completed,* by joining the leash to the collar as you've been told. Do not substitute anything stronger than the store string, regardless of the size of your dog. We do not want a string strong enough to hold your dog — you should no longer have to hold him, nor even lightly cue him — but only strong enough to serve as a symbol of a relationship you have established.

When collar and leash are linked with the string, give a heel command, and go on a "cook's tour" around the premises, using a few random distractions en route.

House doors, gates, and car doors are particularly good places to check and see if he sits automatically. Give him a trial on all the exercises learned thus far, including a change of pace on the heeling. If your dog does them all and seems to take the temptations as cues to be even more attentive, it shows that you have taken him past the "point of contention" and have laid the groundwork for the wonderful accomplishments to begin with the next lesson.

If your dog failed to perform any of the exercises, if the string broke, if you side-stepped or leaned to keep the string intact, or if you gave double commands, your position is not one of authority. You are not the boss. *You had better return to the practicing of your leash work until you are.*

When you and your dog are able to pass this string test, there is one thing you will have learned — an important thing: "the meaning of training a dog so that he comes to take the strongest distraction as another reason for thinking of you. . . ."

And then you'll be ready for the next lesson.

Roy Roger's "Bullet" was one of the dogs that participated in a "Fun Frolic for Dogs" to raise funds for the children at Casa Colina Home for Crippled Children. (*Photo by C. Lydon Lippincott*)

Lesson XIV

THE THROW-CHAIN

It is true that obedience is most needed during times of emergency. It is equally true that obedience, like all insurance, must be obtained before you need it. On this premise, our training has progressed to a point where your dog, when on line or leash, takes distractions as a cue to be even more attentive to you, having found that it is at such moments that you are most likely to act.

The time has come for him to learn that you can act with something besides a leash. However, one of the most important progressions of dog training is the proper transition from on-leash to off-leash control, so keep that leash on your dog until you're told when and how to take it off. Right now, we'll use the leash to introduce your dog correctly to the throw-chain.

Until told differently, don't even have the chain in your hand unless the dog is on the leash. While the throw-chain will cause an amazing response, it is instruction through the leash that determines the pattern of that response.

Before you begin the lesson, arrange for two temptations in your training area or, better yet, take your dog to a fresh area. If possible, have someone go along as your helper.

Whether you score a miracle or a miss depends on how well you learn and observe each of the rules for using the throw-chain and the principles underlying its use.

First: Don't let your dog see you throw the chain. This should pose no problem. Your dog has eyes at only one end. Throw at the other. There are four reasons for this rule: (a) It's impossible to injure an eye when the chain strikes the dog on the rear. (b) He certainly won't try to dodge the chain if he cannot see it coming. (c) If he doesn't see your throwing motion, the chain will not be associated with a threatening action that would seem a gesture to drive him away. (d) There will be benefits from mystery and surprise if he sees no contributing action on your part.

Second: Don't miss the dog. Be sure you're so close that you won't. There's no need to worry about your ability. Cold mathematics will show that if the leash runs to his neck and he's facing away from you, the dog's rear cannot be very far away. The most important reason for this "no-miss rule" will be emphasized by your own experience. Simply stated, he won't know you *can* miss him if you don't. Have no wild ideas about getting someone else to throw the chain for you. Many who say they are unable to throw have tried this stunt only to find that they end up with a confused dog.

Third: Don't let him see you pick up the chain. Your dive to grab it would show him that you have only one and that you are emotionally and physically off-balance without it. That's why you have someone along. Have your helper quietly pick up the chain and place it in your throwing hand, which should be held behind your back to receive the chain. While your dog is well able to follow this roundabout method, the system makes for more poise and proficiency on your part. And if no one is around to help you? Simple. Just leave the dog tied behind a wall or building while you pick up the chain. Or, better still, use several chains, mark where they fall, and then collect them all at once. Two or three chains may give an opportunity for another shot that could be missed if you had only one. A four-inch strip of cloth tied to a chain makes it easy to find even in high grass.

When you are certain you know all the rules and reasons, bring your dog into the training area and, holding only the loop of the leash, release him from command with an "okay." Regardless of whether you're right-handed or left-handed, hold the leash so that your throwing hand will be free to handle the chain, which should be clenched so snugly that it will not rattle.

Let your dog relax and enjoy himself on the full length of the leash if he chooses. In fact, go with him so that the leash will not tighten; as you do so, maneuver so that you stay directly behind him.

When your dog is deeply occupied with a distraction or something else of interest, it is time for you to act. Act in a fair and proper order.

Since you gave him his break, it would be unfair and cruel to correct before calling him. Call him in a normal way. If you "overpower" him with volume, you might waste an opportunity for correction. If the dog turns from the point of interest and starts toward you, complete the recall and finish in the usual manner, and praise him.

If he delays as much as one-half second in his response to the command, throw the chain sharply at his rear. Sharply. It will not hurt him unless you toss, lob, or shot-put it so slowly that he has time to turn his face to the impact. Also, if the chain is thrown slowly, he may have time to walk out of its way. When the chain strikes his rear, reel the leash in swiftly and sit the dog in front of you. Postpone the finish until you've given him the most convincing praise possible. After the finish, take one step with the dog at heel and then release him with another "okay."

As before, do not let the leash interfere with his pleasure as you try, quietly, to steer his course back toward the same temptation.

It's now that you may get your shock. That

same dog who has been jerked, shoved, and shamed away from such temptations with no avail now, even though not under command, might shun the situation where he had been corrected only once with the throw-chain. But keep trying. Let your relaxed attitude show him that you have no objection to his "going visiting," which, in truth, you haven't. Your concern begins only when he dares to delay a half second in his response to your recall command.

You may be very lucky and almost immediately get a second opportunity to use the chain. More likely you'll have to wait at least five minutes before his renewed interest will lead him back into the situation, and longer before he will delay his response to your command. Difficult as it now may be to dull his attentiveness to you, saunter, relax, and keep trying.

While you're relaxing, make certain there is not the tiniest sound from the throw-chain.

Finally, if you are skillful and patient, you should get the second opportunity to use the chain. Be sure that the calling, throwing, pulling, and praising are done in the proper order. The author has often seen a person of confused or compromising nature actually work to make his movements known to his dog, then, in weird order, pull the leash, give the command, throw the chain at the dog's head, and then scramble to pick it up while the dog watches. In obedience classes, this individual can be heard lamenting, "The chain doesn't work with my dog."

If, after you use the chain the second time, your dog will not even face the same distraction, change to another tempting situation. Even in new situations your opportunities for correction may depend on letting the dog become engrossed before calling him, instead of giving the command before his interest has a chance to fully develop.

One half of the session where the throw-chain is introduced should be spent on the throw-chain and half on reviewing previously learned exercises. When you've finished, take your dog to a different area for his after-training break on the long line.

Your first experience with the throw-chain might cause you to wonder why dogs that will ignore the discouragement of a sharp leash correction can be so affected by the slight discomfort caused by the chain. Obviously, the reason must be more psychological than physical.

Parallel your dog's situation with a conceivable experience of your own. If you were to watch an expert archer shoot ten consecutive arrows into a target, would you bet that he couldn't do it on the eleventh try? Or that he couldn't repeat the performance from a ten-foot-greater distance? And why wouldn't you wager? Because you had no previous experience to indicate that he would miss, or that there were any limitations of distance.

Your dog will not bet against you if you do not provide experience that shows him you can miss.

Elementary but often overlooked is this fact that most creatures make their "bets" or decisions by previous experience. Hence, all of those important rules, particularly the one about "not missing." Study them again.

Though there's no great discomfort in the procedure, the fact that you can contact him at a distance is mysterious and impressive — and amazingly effective. That this effectiveness causes a response in the right direction, when the instinctively distasteful "throwing at a dog" would ordinarily drive him away, is predetermined by the leash control and then justified in the mind of the dog by the praise you give him. When the response has been justified often enough, it becomes a trait of the dog's conduct and of benefit to his character. And while the appeal of the "right thing" is increasing, the appeal of the "wrong thing" is diminishing. The dog is changing. It is as true of the dog, as of yourself, that each time a temptation is overcome, it is overcome more easily.

If you have one of those unusual dogs that reacts to the throw-chain in a frightened manner, keep on using it. It would be a disastrous thing to stop using it or to use it in a watered-down way. Recall the many situations in which you have been that seemed startling and unfair, but which, through constantly pleasant experience, become no longer startling, but actually inviting. And, after all, it's the dog's decision. If he does nothing to cause you to throw the chain, he'll be getting praise in its place. Would you pity a sore-footed man who insists on running barefoot through briars? There is only one way in which the throw-chain, properly used, could cow your dog. That is when his "pitiful cringing," whether real or phony, "cons" you or a soft-headed member of the family into commiserating with him so that your coaxing and tears convince him that, indeed, he's just had a most unusual and terrifying experience and his fears or "nerves" are perfectly normal. They're not. And neither are you, if you think you can beef up his spine with syrup.

Two days after you begin to use the throw-chain to correct his disobedience on the recall, you can start to use it to increase your dog's reliability in heeling.

Hold the leash so that your throwing hand is kept free for action. A "right-hander" can hold the leash in his left hand, thumb in loop, in a way almost identical with the regular right-hand heeling grip, but with a little more slack so the dog will have opportunity to disobey.

Now, with the leash arranged and the chain

bunched and ready for throwing, give an ordinary heel command and start walking. Avoid any sharp turns or emphatic maneuvers which would cause the dog to be particularly attentive. Keep walking casually along toward any area which you think would invite the dog to drift away from the proper heel position.

Obviously, if his drifting should cause him to lag behind, you could not use the chain — he would see you throw.

The throw-chain should never be used to correct lagging. And don't try to get around the rule by having someone else throw the chain. However, if you play your dog against the point of interest in such a way that he angles away from your side, there will be a split second in which you can throw. And that's long enough for an alert and ready handler. The problem of throwing is even simpler if the dog's interest takes him out ahead of you so that his rear is exposed.

When the moment comes, throw. Hold your mouth shut. Keep on walking. You told him to heel when you started moving, so why should you repeat the command?

And if he should break, why should you call him? He was at heel, and heeling has nothing at all to do with the recall.

If, when hit with the chain, he moves back to "pleasant haven" of his own volition or if your movement snubs him back into line, praise him without breaking your stride. You can have a helper get the chain, or walk the dog around the corner and tie him up while you retrieve it. Naturally, the relative positions of you and your dog, while heeling, will provide fewer opportunities to throw than you will have on the recall exercise. This means you will have to work more carefully to observe the rules. Take courage from the fact that all the while his attentiveness is denying you opportunity for correction, he's getting loads of practice in "being good." So there is no justification for hurrying into throwing in a manner that would violate the rules for the throw-chain's use. Be careful.

When your dog has reached the point where he is very respectful of your ability to contact him at a distance, you can begin to use the throw-chain on a third type of situation: as a correction for wild charging, inside and out. An example of each should be sufficient to demonstrate how useful the chain can be.

Outdoors, a common source of embarrassment to his master is the wild-eyed, indiscriminate charger who rushes the gate or streaks along the fence, gouging a groove through the landscape. In contrast to a qualified watchdog, this gouger is likely to charge the same mailman or garbage man who has been serving the house for years. Probably his pathetic master's futile efforts to head him off have increased the dog's speed and zest for the chase. From his owner's vocal and physical exercises, he has learned two things: The master doesn't like it, and he is too slow to do anything about it. Your dog may soon learn there is something that isn't "too slow."

By now you know that the working premise of dog training is a situation which will give the dog an opportunity to show his disobedience and, at the same time, provide you with a definite opportunity to correct him.

If it's the garbage man your dog charges, meet the man a couple of doors down the street and arrange for him to make five or six noisy arrivals spaced a minute apart. You'll find that when he learns your purpose, he'll be most cooperative. He'll be a grateful man. Be sure to have your longe line fastened to your dog's collar before the man's first arrival.

The many times you've watched the dog travel his frenzied path should tell you just where to stand to get a shot at his rear or side. Yes — obsessed as he is — you can risk a shot at his side as he tears past.

Don't call him before you throw. It's not a recall. He's to be punished for doing something that a hundred ineffectual reprimands have told him is wrong. Besides, you want him to refrain from chasing garbage men even at times when you're not around to call him.

Watch, when he starts his run, for that right

moment. Then throw. Grab the line and snatch him back to where you are standing. Don't praise him. The jerk is to show him that while you can't outrun him, you can interrupt his idiotic dash from a distance and make him end up in front of you.

After this first "interruption," it may be that he won't turn his attention from you until it appears that the garbage man has faded from sight and sound. If necessary, disappear from the dog's point of view so he'll relax before the man's second arrival. When the rattling and clanging announces the man's return, casually drift back into position for action. As before, throw when you can, then grab and reel in the line. After a few repetitions of the "arrival, chase, and chain routine," your dog might appear to lose interest in garbage men.

Tell the garbage man to give it everything he's got on the clattering and banging so that the activities are as inviting as possible. Let the man know that he should not watch the dog as though directing his activities at him in a teasing way. When your dog has been worked to a point where he will no longer show an interest, stage a few more arrivals to give him an opportunity to practice being good.

Possibly it will take several sessions with the garbage man before your dog is cured of harassing this familiar caller.

If you have one of those rare dogs who can only be discouraged by heavier artillery than the throw-chain, rest easy. When you read the lesson on problems, you will learn how to use equipment that will bring about the dog's conversion in a matter of moments.

The damage he does outside is small in comparison to the financial havoc that a charger can achieve indoors. Here, upon hearing the approach of a familiar service man, a well-practiced dog can roll up a throw rug, knock over a small table, and damage blinds or drapes in a single floor-scratching scramble.

The mailman's arrival makes an exemplary situation in which to demonstrate how well we can cope with this problem of charging inside the house. The mailman, like the garbage man, will brim with gratitude when you ask for his cooperation. After all, the sounds have made him expect the dog to break out through the wall of the house at any time.

Arrange to signal the man with a porchlight or the movement of a curtain when you want him to approach and start the action.

If you have furniture that might catch and interfere with your long line, use a piece as short as six or eight feet. Without a knot or hand-hold in the end, it will slide right over things without catching.

When your dog is equipped and relaxed, ease into a strategic position, and be ready with your throw-chain. You will handle the chain and line on these indoor setups exactly as you did the outdoor situation. This means timing your throw to hit the dog when he starts his charge and using the line to flip him away from the direction of his rush so fast he'll practically face himself in midair. The more startling, uncomfortable, and conclusive the experience, the greater its benefits. (Note: If you have to retrieve the chain yourself, tie the dog in another room while you pick it up.)

Give your dog the advantage of as many "approaches" as possible. Keep in mind that when he's denying you opportunities for correction, he's getting more and more practice in "being good." Again, it may take several sessions with the chain and line before he swears off mailmen, but repeat the performance until the sound of the man's approach causes your dog to turn from that direction as though suffering acute nausea.

Ridiculous as it seems, many inexperienced trainers are slow to adopt the principles that apply in one situation to another similar situation. What works in the case of the garbage man and mailman also applies in the case of the gas man, milkman and other callers who come to your house so regularly that any discriminating dog should know their presence is legitimate.

Work carefully and consistently on the three aforementioned types of situations in which the throw-chain might be used for correction

— recall, heeling, and charging — and add new distractions as your dog grows in reliability. Be equally consistent in taking advantage of any situations that develop without your help. To work successfully in those situations which you set up and then to let the dog get away with a charge because a chance opportunity has caught you flat-footed is to cancel out much of your good work. In short, keep that line on the dog when he's in the house and at such times as there is the least possibility of someone approaching to tempt him. And keep that throw-chain in a handy pocket. Lay for him.

The time spent each day for working with the throw-chain on the problems of the recall, heeling, and charging will probably average about fifteen minutes. Spend an equal amount of time on your regular, routine exercises in a definite effort to increase your dog's accuracy and reliability. Your dog will be rigorously tested for these qualities at the start of the next chapter.

Within two weeks from the time when you began work with the throw-chain, you should feel like wagering that no distraction will tempt your dog. That is, unless you have that "one-in-a-hundred" dog that is so tough he ignores the chain. As has been said, we'll discuss his type a bit further along in the lesson on problems. You may be certain there is something he won't ignore.

Lesson XV

THE LIGHT LINE

The ease and certainty with which a dog, trained past the point of contention on leash, may be made to perform with equal reliability when free of restraint is sometimes a source of embarrassment to those who had fearfully approached what they thought was a gamble. Properly achieved, the control of an unrestrained dog is so simple that they are embarrassed because they "didn't think of it." Yet, simple though it is, there is an occasional person who does not grasp the underlying principle and so fails to get the fullest benefits from the technique.

Just why the method works on a dog is more easily understood when you see that it would work on a person — even a very intelligent person. So you will have the best possible understanding of our procedure, borrow an "intelligent person" — preferably one who's good at mathematics, such as an engineer or accountant — and we'll see how he can cope with the principles we'll use.

The implement that bridges the gap between control on the leash or longe and control when the dog is physically free will be a piece of light line, different in appearance from anything you have used thus far, particularly in its length. It should be very strong, very long, and very light: So strong that your dog couldn't possibly break it; so long that, regardless of his great speed and your slowness, you would have no difficulty in grabbing the trailing end; and so light that its weight and length would be almost imperceptible — certainly offer no discouragement to the dog's attempts to run.

You'll be surprised to find, with a little investigation, that there are lines made of newly developed materials that have tremendous strength and little weight. For example, there are saltwater fishing lines of very small diameter that can stop the wildest rush of the biggest dog. Lines that will hold the medium- and small-size dogs are not much larger than string. To make absolutely certain the line is correct in strength and weight, question a fisherman or other expert.

As to length, you're the sole judge. If you have a fast dog that you feel is going to try to bolt away and you are mentally or physically slow, get a line a hundred feet long or longer. Remember this: You can get a line that's hundreds of yards long, and two or more can be tied together. Certainly, then, neither your dog's speed nor your slowness poses a real problem.

If your line is bright and easily seen, dull it down by dipping it in dye or leftover coffee.

Leave your dog in the yard, bring your

"intelligent human," the line, and a pocket knife, and we'll go into an open area for a few interesting experiments. Start by unwrapping about ten feet of line from your roll and then walking along with the ten feet dragging on the ground. With its smoothness and small size, you'll hardly feel its drag. Now unwrap another ten feet; walk and try to feel the difference. Chances are you'll be unable to feel any more drag from the longer length than from the shorter. Unwrap another ten feet and walk. Again, the additional length has caused no difference in the feel of the line.

Keep firmly in mind the fact that it's impossible for a person or a dog to estimate the length of a very light line from the feel of its drag.

Next, ask your "intelligent human" to face straight ahead while you drop a noose of string over his head. Cut about thirty feet of line from the ball and string the thirty feet straight out behind your friend. Now, ask him to try his best to run away while you try to grab the line and stop him. The answer will be a "no." Let's look at the thing from his viewpoint. You didn't tell him how long the line is; he couldn't estimate its length when he saw it wrapped in a ball, and even if he should whirl around to look at it, he would need considerable time to locate its end. And, as you found, the drag on the ground will tell him nothing.

So how could he possibly know how long the line is, or how much time you would have to make your grab? How can he possibly figure his chances for running away from you?

Now your helper, even though he may be a brilliant engineer, is standing there with a line on his neck, and, for all he knows, it may be a hundred yards long and strong enough to hold a bull. And he doesn't want to find out the hard way.

After he's had a few of the right experiences, neither will your dog want to find out the hard way.

"But," you're sobbing, "what happens when the line comes off?"

Let's find out. Again we'll use your human helper. After you assure him that you have no intention of stretching his neck, ask him to walk about, letting the line drag from his neck. Walk along about ten feet behind him and, without letting him know what you're doing, quietly cut the line.

Ask him to run. He won't. Because there is so little feel to the drag, he won't be aware that he now has a short line and a good chance of getting away. And, after your dog has had the right experiences, neither will he.

To go further, enough of the right experiences can make both a human and a dog refuse to run from you even though the line is completely off from their necks.

Now that we've proved that neither man nor dog can calculate his chances of running away when he doesn't know the length or strength of the line on his neck, let's see how we'll use the line to give your dog those "right experiences."

If you are going to get the fullest benefit from your first session with the light line, it's most important that it be fastened to the dog properly. Keep in mind the "why" as well as the "how" of the procedure.

Stretch your line out conveniently in the training area, making sure that it is free of knots and snarls that would offer resistance when dragged. Once more, the length of the line must be your decision. No one else knows how fast you think and run in comparison with your dog.

When you bring your dog into the area, have both the tab and leash fastened to his collar. (The illustration on page 265 shows a properly attached tab.) Spend a few minutes reviewing with the dog on leash. Arrange to finish the practice with an automatic sit at one end of the line.

Carefully, so as not to inform the dog of what you are doing, tie the end of the line to the loop in the tab with a good, firm knot. One of the several reasons that we use the tab should now occur to you. By wearing the device during some of his leisure time, your dog has become accustomed to the tug of its swinging and bobbing and will hardly notice the additional tug of the dragging light line. In case you make him suspicious with a big, fumbling production of tying the knot, a bit of heeling and sitting while you still hold the leash will make him forget the line is attached.

After a few starts and stops, place your throw-chain in the proper hand for action. Remove the leash, being very careful not to entangle it with the line and cause a "reminding tug." Throw the leash a few feet out in front of the dog. Give a heel command and start walking.

If you are lucky, the discarded leash and weightlessness of the line will give him such an unrestrained feeling that he'll break, expose his rear, and give you your opportunity to use the chain.

Throw. Then get one foot, or both feet, on the line to slow it down before you grab it. This is not difficult when the dog's break occurs from the heel position, because the line's length should give even a slow handler time to grind his heel down upon it. To grab the line bare-handed, before it has been slowed down, is like stroking a power saw. A thin glove is a good added precaution.

Reel in the line without a word as you keep right on walking. However, it's almost certain that your surprised dog headed back to your side the moment the tightening line told him that he wasn't quite as free as he felt.

After all, your groundwork with leash and chain had taught him the whereabouts of "pleasant haven," and the line showed him you needed no leash to make sure he'd get there.

At this time you will feel very thankful that your groundwork took him past the point of argument, for, unbreakable though it is, the light line does not give the good hand grip necessary to setting a pattern with an argumentative dog.

Definitely stated, the line is an unfailing assurance that a dog will perform in a pattern that has been established: It is neither a comfortable nor an effective implement for establishing a pattern. Your leash should have done the establishing weeks ago.

When your throw-chain has been recovered, reattach your leash and then repeat the procedure of holding the leash and line together, as you do starts and stops. By thus focusing his attention on the leash, you will recreate the feeling of freedom when the leash is removed and thrown in front of him.

Possibly, his first experience made such an impression that when the leash is again thrown on the ground, he'll check his inclination to break and will be quite content to heel respectfully along beside you. This is the moment to stop and, regardless of how he sits, show him with sincere praise that he's doing exactly the right thing in obeying as though you held the leash.

Whether he shows this cooperativeness the first time the leash is removed or after experiencing correction with the chain, make certain you show this approval.

Do not make the mistake of asking the dog to heel interminably without telling him he's doing the right thing. This would confuse him, and when he finally breaks, he might be doing so because he didn't know what you wanted. If you praise him for a little heeling, he'll be apt to give you a lot more; then, when temptation finally causes him to break, your correction will be justified because he's experienced the pleasant results that came from doing the right thing. So praise him now and then as you keep working and waiting for that second opportunity to correct.

Whether you get the one correction or many, when you've worked as long as fifteen minutes on the light line procedure, put the throw-chain back into your pocket, remove the line, and with both the leash and tab fastened to the collar, use the remainder of your training period to increase accuracy and reliability by practicing the routine exercises.

While you're practicing, it may help you to keep in mind that you are using a wonderful formula for controlling a dog's attitude toward a situation. This is the almost magical effect of utilizing the feeling of competence and confidence that comes from doing a familiar exercise by backwashing the feeling into a preceding situation wherein the dog felt less competent and familiar. To follow the new and strange with a review of the familiar can do much to establish your dog's proper attitude for the new thing he is learning, which in this case was response when off-leash. Deliberately use this principle to make your dog confident and happy in his work.

After your training period is finished, replace the leash with your longe line and give your dog an "okay" release and a bit of relaxation as the two of you saunter around the area.

Later on in his training, when you feel complete confidence, your longe will be replaced by the light line during the after-training break period. To make the change too early would be to invite a lineburn on your hands.

Your dog has done a good job and deserves a break period uninterrupted by distractions or commands. As it is, his experience with the light line may have left him so concerned that you'll have to work to get him to relax. He'll learn, eventually, that the line not only signifies authority but can provide fun as well.

Put him back into his yard when the break is over and leave him alone for a while.

It may be that instead of performing in a manner similar to that described, your dog acted differently. You could have made a fumbling production out of tying the line, entangled it with the leash, or in some other way aroused his suspicions so that he never for a moment felt free enough to run. Or possibly he is one of those that stands still when the leash comes off, having stopped himself by stepping on the line. In any case, the problem is the same: The dog must be made so familiar with the presence of the line that he will forget or ignore it. You can accomplish this by giving him lots of walking on leash while he drags the line, which should be tied to the tab in the usual way. This will accustom him to moving even though the line slides between his toes or brushes on his legs. After a few of these "conditioning sessions," he'll hardly be aware of the line and tab. Then you can return to the main project of using the line to establish off-leash control.

After two days of using the light line to assure response on the off-leash heeling, you should have enough confidence to use it in one of those situations where the dog is at a greater distance from you. You will find it particularly useful for correcting the dog that does a good sit-stay and recall, even at considerable distance, as long as the longe line is fastened to his collar in the manner described earlier but, when that authoritative weight is gone, sits staring confusedly.

Here's a way to blast that "mental vapor-lock." Before placing your dog for a recall, lay out your line so that it can run from where you plan to leave him to a point a few feet straight behind him, and from that point circle back to where you intend to stand. Fasten the tab to his collar; then bring him into the area on leash and stop where you planned to leave him. Try to join the line to the tab so smoothly that he will not even know you are doing it.

Because the line is laid out to circle around behind him, there will be nothing visible in the dog's immediate foreground to make him expect a setup. Place him on a sit-stay, then move to the other end of the line and casually pick it up.

Because the operation has been much smoother than if you had fumbled around at laying out the line after it was tied to the tab, your dog will probably not be aware that you are prepared to correct him should he, without the reminder of the longe line or the leash, hesitate in coming when called.

After facing him for a few seconds, give a recall command. If he responds promptly, praise him as he starts toward you; thus he's receiving praise for his decision to come, not merely for sitting in front of you. Remember, there is a difference between praising and coaxing.

If he doesn't respond promptly, jump backward in a way that tightens the line in an unforgettable jerk.

Properly given, the correction should convince him that he had better move when he hears the command, even though he hasn't been reminded by the weight of the leash or the longe line. Repeat this setup a few times each day until the dog responds promptly.

If your emphasis on a fast response causes him to anticipate and come before he is called, the line will again be an asset. It can stop him cold if he tries to run off or bolt, as you charge back to grab the tab and make your stay correction. As you grab, you'll realize that along with making the dog forget the line, the tab makes a very good handsaving handle. Your persistent efforts with the line will show your dog that regardless of the absence of weight on his collar or the distance from you, he had better stay until called and then come immediately.

While the throw-chain can never be used in situations such as the aforementioned, where the dog is facing you, it can be used to settle the hash of the smart aleck who takes off in a wrong direction when called. **Again, caution: Don't ever throw if he runs before he is called. This means that he broke the stay, and only the usual sit-stay correction should be used.**

If your dog is an "artful dodger" who bears down on you and then scoots to one side, or if he makes a game of shooting past you and circling back, tag his fanny with the chain as he flashes past. This, and the solid jolt of the line, will make him believe that the best way to make sure his rear is away from you is to keep his head toward you.

On the more important informal recall, where the dog is called away from a distraction you have provided, or an emergency that occurs naturally, the throw-chain will be used in conjunction with the light line. Follow exactly the same procedure as when you used the chain in conjunction with the leash and heavy line. Of course, experience gained from working with the heavier equipment should have increased your proficiency with the chain, and made such a pattern of the dog's response that he reacts without any thought of argument.

The difference and advantage of the lighter equipment is the fact that it is the bridging step to the technique of controlling the dog when he is entirely free of restraint. The previously discussed case of the indiscriminate charger who harasses the garbage man, mailman, and other familiar callers will also require work on the light line if off-leash reliability in those situations is to be achieved.

Again, the technique of using the line in combination with the chain will follow the pattern of the earlier work with the heavier equipment. Naturally, the increased length of the line over the other equipment will provide control at a greater distance. He can't tell the length by the weight, so set up your situations in such a way that his mad dash takes him quite a distance before the line and chain remind him that there's absolutely no way of telling how far away you can control him. If he's charging inside the house, you may find it convenient to use a shorter line than the one you use outside.

To increase your dog's reliability on the sit-stay and down-stay, you can quietly attach the line to the tab before you remove the leash and soon convince him that he had better hold his stays even when he's not reminded by the weight of the leather and snap.

Within a week after you begin to use the light line, you'll find that your dog has changed. He will no longer disobey the heel and recall commands. The greater the distractions you provide to encourage his "charging," the more he seems to turn his attention back to you. At least, that's the way it is when he's on the line. You wonder what would happen in those same situations if the line were not on him.

There's a way you can arrange for a preview of what will happen when the line finally comes off. First, make sure that your dog has had sufficient periods of the right kind of work to make him infallible when he's on the line. Before bringing him out for his trial, equip yourself with a small scissors or knife. To fumblingly untie the line from the tab in the nervous manner of one removing the detonator from an explosive is to tell the dog that you are no longer confident and neither your commands nor actions are to be respected.

Work with the full length of light line and the throw-chain on the heeling exercise until his attitude tells you that distractions are only making him more attentive. Now is the time to stoop over and, without any fumbling around, reach back and cut the line about four feet from the dog's collar. Let both ends lie where they fall. Give a command and start off with your usual confidence.

Your dog will respond to your command and actions in the usual way.

"Why shouldn't he?" you protest. "There's still some line on him."

And then, as you walk along, it hits you. Physically, that four feet of line is hardly better than nothing. It would be almost impossible to grab that short line in time to stop him from bolting, but your dog is walking along as resignedly as though it were forty feet long and his chances of breaking were nil. He does not take pencil and paper and compute his chances of outrunning you, considering the factors of your relative speed against the reduced length of the line. A dog's arithmetic is not that good. He does not even turn to look at the end of the line.

And, aware of the consequences he previously experienced, no properly trained dog would ever dare to run without being certain of the length of line attached to his collar. For that matter, neither would a human. Not even an accountant or an engineer.

The principles of the light line never fail. At times, a trainer, through laziness or lack of imagination, will fail in his application of those principles.

In your command there was no quaver that would let your dog know that you weren't fully prepared to cope with him. Come to think of it, you didn't feel like quavering. You didn't feel a lack of confidence. Strangely enough, though it was only four feet long, that line not only did something for the dog, it also did something for you.

Rather mysterious, isn't it?

You'll come to find that the line will keep doing that "something" for you and your dog when it's only five inches long. And when it's gone.

You've now seen how your dog responds on four feet of line. That was to demonstrate the method of your progress. In the actual practice of good training, we wouldn't reduce the working length of the line to four feet in one step. Rather, we'd cut a few feet from the dragging end every few days providing, of course, that the dog continued to reach new levels of reliability when tested in situations of increased distraction. This testing will prevent you from making the serious mistake of reducing the line length too fast.

The next session, after you've had your "preview" on the four-foot length, should feature practice with the light line on all previously discussed exercises, in addition to your leash work.

This means practice on the full length of line, not the four-foot piece.

At this time, which generally comes after three weeks of working with the throw-chain and one week after beginning to use the chain in conjunction with the light line, we're going to add something to the training procedure.

You will recall how you were instructed to finish your training periods by letting your dog drag the longe around for awhile as he relaxed, uninterrupted by distraction or command from you. You were probably pleased to see how quickly your dog came to enjoy these "breaks." The procedure blended into a companionship that is most enjoyable for you and your dog. You can both benefit still further from these interludes.

It is now that we will start giving the dog his break periods on the light line instead of on the longe. In addition to the regular aftertraining breaks, two or three times a week attach the line to your dog's collar and without any preliminary work take him on a sauntering walk in an area he will enjoy. It would be a special treat if one period should be a long hike on a weekend, with a car ride to and from the location.

It would add to your confidence if, occasionally, you were to grab the line to enforce a recall or to get your dog heading your way if a stray dog or cat beckoned his attention. Be careful never to restrain him. Use the slack and a right-about to bump him and emphasize the merit of heading your way.

But primarily try to make your dog feel that the purpose of these walks is your mutual pleasure, not his training.

You now have the information necessary to use your light line and throw-chain as a bridging step to off-leash obedience in the exercises of heeling and recalling and in the correction of problems that have to do with bolting or charging.

You have seen how the line can cause a dog to resign himself to holding a stay position by showing him the consequences of trying to run from correction when something, often quite unnoticeable, just might be tied to his collar.

You have found how your dog, already appreciative of the aftertraining breaks on the line, can be made much happier by the combination of control, confidence, and pleasure that the light line brings.

The light-line work, which should occupy about a third of your training time, will provide control and mutual confidence when your dog is at a distance. The remainder of the time, spent on leash work, will increase the dog's accuracy and promptness. The leash, with its positive grip, provides such an authoritative correction that it discourages arguments and gives a great many opportunities for praise, thereby progressively instilling in the dog a greater compliancy of mind.

It is the function of the light line to show the dog that he can be held accountable for the qualities of control and character gained through the leash work, even when the leash is not present.

Within two weeks from the day you begin work with the line, you'll find that both you and your dog have changed. You now feel very confident that he will obey under any condition on a line which your week of "testing and shortening" has reduced to two-thirds of its original length.

Exactly how long is the line at this time? That you'll have to gauge against your own confidence and the work you've done. If your confidence has shortened along with the line, you'll know you've cut too much too soon. Play it safe. Let your confidence be your guide.

From this two-week point on, you may be able to reduce the length of the line gradually, until by the end of the fourth week, you feel qualified to work the dog with only one foot of line hanging from the tab, or a few inches, or nothing.

Possibly, your dog may be one of those that needs the influence of the tab and one or two feet of line even after a month of line work. Or it could be that he is one of the erratic type that appears reliable but is ready to take a tight situation or tension in your voice as an inspiration to try to outwit you. If the shortness of your line has enabled him to outmaneuver you, sneak a long line back onto him, put him back in the same situation, get the same tension into your voice, and then, when he breaks, give him an experience that he'll never forget. By dumping him end over end after he's been tagged with the chain, you may make an indelible impression that could sometime save his life. It is probable that the influence of the throw-chain will have him back at your side even before you can begin to tighten the line.

After this "experience," lay for him by alternating between short and long lines, giving him the greatest distractions when he's on the long piece. Another valuable procedure is to let the dog drag the light line around in the yard or house and then open the door and bring him under command. He's almost certain to bolt out a few times and give you a chance to use the chain. Eventually, an open door will be a cue to think of you.

Regardless of your own abilities and the peculiarities of your dog, one thing is certain: The line will give you an unfailing means with which you will ultimately accomplish his off-leash control. What an accomplishment! Not only will your dog obey your commands off leash, but you will have laid the foundation for the solving of problems that might occur later.

THE RIGHTISTS

In his book *Animal Liberation*, Peter Singer makes a strong case for changing our attitude toward the treatment of animals we keep for food and other purposes. He has been the inspiration and source of facts for most of the groups that are commonly referred to as animal rightists. Because many of Singer's thoughts were expressed rationally, it is difficult for the public to understand the actions of some of the terrorists who have attached themselves to groups that might be sincerely interested in the welfare of animals.

To understand the actions of individuals who will destroy laboratories and research programs involved in projects that could ease the suffering of both animals and humans, one must be aware of a peculiar appetite that motivates them. Such a person is convinced that each animal he meets is suffering from a need about which no one else, not even the owner, knows. Even when there is no reason for such concern, commiserators appear to get a sensual satisfaction out of a cooing, baby-talking approach to an animal — generally a dog.

Motion-picture animal handlers believe that the most aggressive of these commiserators are the women who work in the movie industry — hairdressers, makeup artists, and, yes, some actresses. They are particularly responsive to the plight of a dog who is resting in the security of his familiar crate until it is time for him to work.

Concluding that such confinement must be torturous to an animal, some of these zealots will go as far as to open the crate, then be surprised that the confused animal doesn't want to stay with his liberator and runs away from the area.

Whether confined or not, there are a few things that all animals are in immediate need of, according to the do-gooders. All of them must be in need of water and food. In one personal experience, my partner and I arranged to use the Wire Foxed Terriers we had established as the Asta character on *The Thin Man* on a pilot. It was a cold, foggy morning when I carried my crates onto the stage and then went back out to make sure I had turned off the headlights on my vehicle.

By the time I returned to the stage, a hairdresser had already opened the young dog's crate and had given him a pan of water, which was of no interest to him. When I came on the stage, the dog was running around among the stands that held the reflectors and lights. He saw me and came running to my waiting arms. When I put him back in his crate, he relaxed and sighed, obviously with the secure feeling that he did not have to keep track of me. Had the hairdresser opened the principal dog's crate, she might have been bitten, as he was extremely protective of his restricted space, although Asta was calm and very reliable when working on a set. He had won the American Humane Society's PATSY award for the best animal actor in television, and you may be assured he was well cared for with all the food, water, and other creature comforts he needed.

In recent years, the media has documented an astounding number of terrorist activities by violent members of animal rights groups. Drop by your library and read some of the accounts. You'll be surprised at the prestigious stature of organizations they have attacked and who have learned they must take them seriously and oppose them. And you will see why anyone involved in obedience training and other dog related activities should be familiar with their tactics and how to defeat them.

If a dog yelps while being trained and an accuser enters the scene and threatens the trainer with legal action and will not listen to a rational explanation, he should be told court action will be welcomed. He should know that the dog will be taken to a veterinarian immediately so there will be evidence of the dog's good care if and when you are taken to court, along with other evidence useful again when your lawyer prepares charges of false accusations and harassment. The accuser should be made aware that he can be required to prove his qualifications for his opinion, to substantiate his accusations with some documentable experience and expertise. He should know that employment as a humane officer does not automatically accredit a witness as an expert.

Whether the defense of an individual or a group is being planned, the choice of an attorney is very important. Avoid one whose concern seems to be keeping peace in a community rather than mounting a defense that would blister a humaniac accuser who probably "meant well and was known as a kindhearted animal lover who went about doing good." When a scrappy lawyer is retained, he should know he is expected to challenge any witnesses' claims of experience that would qualify them as creditable judges of animal training and handling. He should be aware that many employed as humane officers were engaged in a wide variety of totally unrelated occupations before they were hired as humane workers. Probably your willingness and careful preparation to do battle will give the accuser a look at the real world and cause him to retract his charges.

The above is more than an example on how to deal with an individual zealot; it is a demonstration of opposition to the anarchy of the animal rights movement. Perhaps you are wondering if you can successfully fight against the "big pressure" by the rightists (use of endorsements by celebrities and emotional appeals in the media).

You can.

As your research will reveal, the attacks of the animal rightists have increased in the level of senseless viciousness. You can help defeat this by bringing their anarchy to the attention of reasonable folks whenever you can. Identify the articles and quote them. And quote from them in letters you send to the editors of your local newspaper. There are still many people with common sense who are opposed to the campaigns of misdirected zealots who try to force a variety of their viewpoints on the larger society.

Dog magazines, club bulletins, and club meetings are some of the many channels for spreading information on a movement that threatens the dog fancy.

Organized opposition is growing as people see the reality and strength of the attacks the rightists make on anything of which they do not approve. Become informed. Lend your support. Dog clubs will welcome your input. The threat to all dog activities is real. Think of all the ways you can oppose the rightists, then work on it.

The American Humane Association presented "Sam" its PATSY Award for top animal picture star of 1959 in recognition of his role in *The Shaggy Dog* and awarded "Asta" its Television PATSY Award for his work in *The Thin Man.* One of the important functions of the American Humane Association is to protect the welfare of animal actors through consultation and advice offered by experienced representatives present during the filming of all pictures featuring animals.

The right kind of training brings control and security to all situations. *(Photo by C. Lydon Lippincott)*

Lesson XVI

DON'T LOSE IT — USE IT

You have spent the training periods of many weeks teaching your dog exercises that are essential to his control, fundamental to future training, and will assist in correcting problems of conduct and character. You are now at a point of decision — a decision that will determine whether you acquire control as infallible in the demanding situations of daily living as you demonstrated among the strong distractions of your formal training periods.

Before your previous success and confidence causes you to dismiss the question with a "Why not?" let's consider the case of the top obedience trial winner who appears faultless during training and competition but seems to revert to an almost undomesticated state on the street or in the home. In the same ring with such a dog may be others who might score lower but maintain their reliable conduct when they leave the ring and whenever they're seen on the street or at home.

This second type debunks the statements of the ignorant who say, "Show obedience is like an act — just a routine." Remember, too, the atmosphere of a dog show is not always the same solidly familiar bedlam. Strange things often happen. The judge is nearly always a stranger. Runaway dogs bolt into the ring. Canvas fences flap and blow down. On the sit-stay and down-stay, the dogs are placed by others they have not seen before. Certainly, the formal obedience ring is a pretty fair test of behavior amidst strong distractions, as you would find if you were to take a dog who is "just kind of trained to mind a little around home" into such a situation.

Why is it, then, that dogs that are so reliable among the distractions of the obedience ring are not equally reliable in the more familiar and less distracting situations of home and street?

Simple enough.

Their masters just didn't work as consistently to create a pattern of unfailing obedience in the other situations as they **were forced to do** to meet the demands of the obedience ring. Obviously, the masters and dogs had the qualities to assure the reliable behavior under extremely tough conditions. Any failure to benefit fully from the dog's training was caused by a decision — or rather, a lack of decision.

If, in your daily living, you use the control developed in your formal training, it will increase and become permanent. If you fail to use it, it will deteriorate and be lost. The decision is whether you will use it or lose it.

Don't depend on luck to give you the opportunities you'll need to transfuse your authority from the training area to the realm of everyday living. Follow the dependable technique of creating tempting situations that you can control. These situations should typify the incidents that are apt to occur in your everyday relationship with your dog.

You will have the most association with your dog at home, so let's start the transfusing process there. But first it would be well to take a look at the mistakes of another handler, which might reflect your own failure. Two things have prevented this handler from fully appropriating to home use the training he has given. First, the home distractions he created were not as similar nor as strong as those that commonly occurred. Second, he failed consistently to take advantage of chance opportunities to use the obedience. Inevitably, his dog quickly sensed the difference between his attitude of preparedness when in the setup situations and his inconsistency when occupied with guests or with other activities.

You can avoid such a person's failures. When you have completed all of the assignments of the preceding lessons, devote ten minutes a day for a week to practicing all of the exercises in every part of the house where your dog might be given a command. So that you are equipped to make the most effective corrections, the dog should be on leash during these periods.

During other times of this week, let him enjoy his home life in such ways as you feel proper, but make certain that the tab, or, if it seems advisable, the tab and a piece of line are fastened to his collar. Have the throw-chain in your pocket, ready for use. Once every hour or so, when you are occupied with tying your shoes, talking on the phone, reading, visiting with company, or some other typical activity, place your dog under command by calling him to you. If he fails to respond, let the speed of your correction prove you are willing to interrupt any activity at any time to back up your command with action.

This procedure will work wonders unless you keep "washing out" your progress by reacting differently when good fortune sends an unplanned occurrence. Throw down the paint brush, jump off the ladder, and, even though a visitor stands open-mouthed, let your correction show the dog that regardless of how busy you are, what position you're in, or how you're interrupted, you'll enforce obedience to your command. And as for being prepared to deal with these unexpected occurrences, I have never heard why, unless he is wearing a bikini bathing suit, a person couldn't have a throw-chain in his pocket.

And please don't tell me a few feet of nylon line fastened to a dog's collar will "catch on everything." It won't.

If your house is filled with knickknacks and you'd like added assurances, use a suitable length of the new plastic-coated clothesline that's on the market. You'll see why it can't snag or tangle. Its slick surface won't give you the hand-grip you'd need for winning an argument with your dog, but he should have been past the arguing point long ago.

By now, your own experience has shown you that when the line has given you control of a situation, a good hand-hold on the tab is your best guarantee of being able to make the final effort necessary to bring the dog into the proper position. Even when you no longer feel the need for the light line, you'll gain much by continuing to have the dog wear the tab in all situations. You'll feel authoritative, knowing that you won't have to seek out the correct collar ring and then handle the dog with an ineffectual grip on the slippery metal. Further, the tab's presence will remind the dog of your authority. Leave it on until you feel your dog is past the need of a correction. As always, you have a responsibility to see that there is no hazard to the dog in the form of objects that could entangle the equipment and choke him.

Once you've decided to do so, there's no great difficulty in applying the authority established in the training area to the situations of the home. The foundation of routine practice in the house, the creating of incidents similar to those likely to occur, and the consistent use of obedience when unplanned occurrences give the opportunity will increase the pleasure and security you and your dog share during your home life.

If properly photographed, the gymnastics of a driver as he copes with a "screwball" dog while driving down a freeway or through downtown traffic might be quite a comedy sequence. That is, it might be a comedy to all but the driver whose neck is at stake. If you, too, are often cast in the dual role of driver and dog fighter, there is an answer to your problem other than leaving your dog at home.

As in the house, the precedent of obedience in the situation is set by practicing routine training in the very place where you will use it. This means in proximity to the car as well as in it. It should be "onleash" practice when the car is standing still, so you are in a position to back up your command with an effective correction regardless of the dog's maneuvers.

Have your car parked in your drive with a door open on each side. Bring the dog, at heel, to a halt within a step of one of the doors. If, instead of sitting automatically, he tries to barge right into the car, you will be in good position for a sit correction. Good car manners begin with entering in the proper way. When he has sat, give him a stay command and have him hold it for at least a minute. Then order him to enter. "Okay, in," seems to convey to the dog that he is released from the stay and can follow the suggested tug of the leash into the car.

In the way that is most convenient for you, maneuver him to that place in the car where you prefer him to ride and put him on a down-stay. Leave him with the leash attached to his collar and stand a few feet from the car, with the doors still open, so you can see if the dog breaks. If he does, move to correct him. After he has held five minutes on this first experience, return, recover your grip on the leash, and bring him from the car by recalling him to a sit position in front of you. After the finish, move off with the dog at heel. Incorporating the car into a pattern of obedience practice will cause your dog to regard it as a place where you might be able to enforce your commands, instead of a situation where he can dazzle you with his footwork, as he's done so often before.

While you wouldn't want your dog to stay rigidly motionless during hours of riding, these long, formal stays are still the best foundation for his later, more relaxed, but controlled conduct in the car.

After a few days, he should enter the car properly on your command, and hold a down-stay for at least twenty minutes, with the doors wide open, while you work at trimming a hedge, or at some other activity which would make him think you're much too preoccupied to do anything about his breaking. Don't let him break the position until you call him from the car and have him finish in the proper manner. **Keep in mind that this formal treatment imparts to the car area that atmosphere and significance created by all of your previous training routines.** The dog is made to feel that the area of the car is indeed a place where he should mind.

After the first few days, you can vary the procedure by entering the car and sitting down while the dog holds a sit-stay outside. If he should attempt to break, jump out and correct him, then return to your seat. When he has held a full minute, call him into the car, place him on a stay, and get out. After he has held for a couple of minutes, call him out with a regular recall and finish. This waiting for the command to get out, as well as to get in, will be a great convenience, and may sometime save your dog's life.

When he's holding well prior to getting in and out of the car, you can introduce the less formal stay, which does not require such a definite position but still keeps the dog in that area of the car you desire. Your longe line will be useful for this job. Bring the dog at heel to the car in the usual manner. After the automatic sit and stay near the door, give him an "okay in." Leave the car doors open and your mouth shut. Don't tell him to stay, but if he leaves that area where you want him to remain, grab the longe and pile him back to where he should be. The line will be long enough to foil him if he tries to dart past you, go out the other door, or jump over the seat.

Let your jerk take him all the way back, and he'll soon learn that, though you didn't tell him to stay, he had better not leave his "riding area" until you tell him to do so. He will learn this in the same way a dog learns to stay in one room of a house or a farm dog learns to stay away from certain sections of a barn: by the bad consequences of his action.

If you have a "geared" or restless dog, he may need the restraint of the formal stays for several days before you go to the relaxed control that only required him to stay in an area. On both types of control, the dog will be made more reliable if you have animals and other temptations brought into the vicinity of the open doors. Now is the time — when the car is motionless and you can correct him — to subject the dog to such distractions.

Now for the next step, which is dealing with the dog when the car is in motion. Get someone to drive for you so you can move right in if the dog gets out of line. As always, have your dog wait for your command to enter the car. If you think he needs the stabilizing effect, put him on a formal sit-stay or down-stay, and as your helper drives along, make sure that he holds it. If your previous training has provided enough distractions to make him solid on his stays, your task shouldn't be difficult. Otherwise, you'll get plenty of exercise twisting and leaning as you bounce him back to where he should be. Remember, even though he may not have been on a formal stay, you can still snatch him back to the place where you want him to remain. Act, don't talk, and he'll soon know he'll be more comfortable in his own area.

Give him a few of the short trips with someone else driving; then, if his attitude seems right, head for an untraveled road, change places with the driver, and convince the dog that you will turn to correct him even when you're occupied with driving. On a quiet road, with your helper ready to grab the wheel, you'll be reasonably safe in whirling around for a correction.

Your program of training and practice will soon make your dog a better traveling companion. Be sure to hold your gains by guarding against sloppy handling on your part. Consistently require your dog to enter the car properly, keep his own place, and leave only on command and under full control.

Naturally, the precept of doing some foundation training in the same area where you might sometime need to control the dog applies to those situations in your yard and away from home. As you were reminded earlier, the statement that you "don't want the dog to leave the place" doesn't eliminate the possibility that someone might leave the gate open or you might have to take your dog with you, if only to the veterinarian's. Leash laws and regulations against dogs running at large can best be observed by the owners of those trained dogs that, when accidentally given their liberty, can be brought back under control. So with the dog on leash, practice the routine exercises in the yard, in all types of street situations, in stores and other places, until he seems relaxed and reliable regardless of the situation.

Since much of your away-from-home work might involve the use of the car, use the opportunities to emphasize that when you stop, he should never come through the door, except on command and under control. Permit no moment of horseplay or indecision while he looks around. Such a moment has caused the death of many dogs.

When you and your dog are performing confidently on these tours, go through the same program, step by step, with your dog on the light line. Be certain that it's long enough and strong enough to keep you capable and confident. This experience will assure you of control and protect the dog against panic when emergencies find him off-leash in strange places.

The light line can be particularly effective in straightening out the bratty dog who, when an open door or gate has provided liberty, dances coyly just out of reach. Set up this situation a few times, preparing carefully with a line long enough to really surprise him. In the case of a dog who is slow to come when called from his liberty in the yard, stack the cards in your favor by leaving the line attached until such time as he's been shown the error of his ways. Then, turn him out on gradually shortened lengths. Don't take the line off completely just because he has responded reliably a hundred times in a row.

Nothing more can be gained by supplying you with any more specific examples of how or where you can use obedience. It is obvious that the methods presented in this book can be applied in all situations where there is a need.

The lesson on "problems" gives information on correcting those dogs whose wickedness is of such a specialized nature as to require something in addition to the character-stabilizing obedience work. So don't let a problem or two distract you from your immediate purpose of giving your dog experience in all of those places where you might have to control him.

And when your work with leash and light line has shown him you're "in charge" anytime, anywhere, be consistent in handling your dog the right way. At home, in the car, away from home, don't lose it — use it.

Margaret Pooley, of the famous Rocky Reach Kennels, obedience trained all of her dogs before they were shown in the conformation classes.

As a significant part of the country's largest obedience program, the Orange Empire Dog Club pioneered street trials. *(Photo by C. Lydon Lippincott)*

PROBLEMS

You have already learned one reason why this book maintains that your dog should be trained in his basic obedience before you make a direct approach to specific problems of conduct and character. Some of those "specific problems" have been corrected by the general benefits of training.

Perhaps not quite so clear is a second reason. This is the fact that, even when it does not completely remedy a situation without direct work on the problem, training in basic obedience makes the success of that direct effort more certain. It is very important to do everything possible to assure success when you first cope with a problem, because to fail on the first attempt is to make the second effort more difficult.

Third, as common sense tells you, it is easier, physically and mentally, to make specific corrections on a dog that has been made more reasonable by obedience training.

There you have three good reasons for completing your basic obedience before trying to use the corrections given in this chapter.

BOLTING, OR RUNNING AWAY

Whether a dog bolts from the house, yard, or car, or runs from the master when on a

recall or heeling, the fault is equally dangerous and maddening. The correction is always
the same in principle. It consists of setting
up situations that give him every incentive
to bolt, and which result in consequences that
make him wish he hadn't.

Whether your "situation" is an accidentally
opened door or the removal of your leash when
in an area where strange dogs happen to be,
the light line should have been quietly attached
to his collar and the throw-chain palmed in
your hand before the "big break" occurs. If the
opportunity is overwhelmingly apparent and
the distraction great enough, he may forget or
disregard the line and bolt. Throw the chain
and use the line to make his experience a
memorable one. Ideally, your jerk on the line
should cause him to swap ends and bounce
back to you, hardly touching the ground.

And what if the dog is so big and tough he
ignores the chain? As was promised earlier,
there is something he won't ignore, no matter
how big and tough and unmanageable he may
be. From a hardware or sporting goods store
get a good slingshot and a few packs of BB
shot. A Wham-O and several other commercial brands will shoot harder and straighter
than the homemade ones that can be made
from today's inner tubes.

If you are one of those unfortunate individuals who have never known the fun of a slingshot,
don't let your lack of experience stop you. Find

out from the sporting goods clerk or an experienced friend how you hold and shoot it. When you've learned the "grip" and "release," put eight or nine BBs into the pouch at one time and shoot the load against a box or can. You'll see that the shot spreads into a pattern that would be quite certain to hit your dog.

Here's the best way to hold the implement while loading and carrying it. Hold the pouch with two fingers behind and the thumb low down on the face so as to prevent the BBs from rolling out before the thumb and forefinger of the other hand pinch the load tight with the shooting grip. It is easy to drop the shot into the pouch by hand or with your mouth. When it's loaded, if you like, you can carry the pouch and the grip in one hand until the moment when the other hand pulls and releases the pouch for the shot. The technique of loading, carrying, and shooting the slingshot with maximum accuracy and force is well worth learning. Your dog, even though he borders on the incorrigible, is not apt to outrun, nor ignore, those BBs. If he does, the small steel balls, such as come packed with the Wham-O slingshot, are procurable at many stores. Even if he has a heavy coat, the recalcitrant dog will not ignore them.

The slingshot, like the throw-chain it replaces, is held in readiness and used at the moment the dog bolts. You won't hit the dog in the eye if you shoot when he's running away, so rear back and let him have it. If you have to really sting him to make him respond when he otherwise might bolt into traffic, console yourself with the fact that the positive control you are establishing may sometime save him from injury or death.

Provide your dog with opportunities to bolt until it seems they only serve to turn his mind back to the light line and you.

And when good fortune causes a friend to open a car door or a gate with your dog in a position to bolt, don't miss your chance because "the line wasn't on him." In the house and out, leave a piece of line on for the influence it exerts, until an open door or gate seems only a cue for the dog to look at you. And even when you reach this point, don't suddenly take it off. Use the technique, explained earlier, of shortening the line bit by bit, corresponding with your own confidence. When the last of the line has been removed, let the dog wear the tab for a while longer. It will serve you well.

Work consistently, using the line to guard against bad breaks, and your dog will come to agree that regardless of "opportunities" and "distractions," he's much better off staying with you.

FENCE RUNNING AND GATE CHARGING

If your dog persists in fence running and

gate charging even after he's been "dusted" repeatedly with the throw-chain, you'll have to resort to the heavy artillery of the slingshot. This is in conjunction with the light line, of course. Whether he runs a fence race with the neighbor's dog, convoys a person along a walk, or runs without a visible provocation, it is your job to give him an incentive and then stake out in a convenient spot.

If you have practiced, you'll be able to give the miscreant quite a surprise. The range and impact of the slingshot is much greater than that of the throw-chain. With a good load of BBs in the pouch, you can fire through an open window and across a yard with an effectiveness that leaves the dog remarkably quiet. When the "quiet" comes, continue to let him drag the line, gradually reducing the length until finally it is lost.

Where landscaping or other physical factors make the use of the slingshot impossible, results can sometimes be obtained by fastening three or four feet of light line to the dog's collar and attaching a "drag" consisting of a piece of two-by-four to the other end. The size of the dog will determine the length of the wood. Three to eight inches seems to cover the range of sizes pretty well. Drive a staple in the middle of the wood or bore a hole so you can attach the line.

When the dog runs, he causes the two-by-four to bounce in a crazy, jerking pattern that will give him some most discouraging whacks. By gradually reducing the size of the drag, some dogs can be brought to the point where a piece of light line or the tab will serve as a reminder of what their running can bring.

If there is danger of the dog becoming entangled and choked, use a line that is strong enough to pull the drag but which will break in an emergency struggle.

STAYING HOME

A surprisingly large number of dogs, if sufficiently grounded in their response to light line and throw-chain, can be taught to stay within the boundaries of an area, even if those boundaries are marked with only a low fence, a hedge, or a flower row.

If you feel that your dog is intelligent and well-grounded in obedience, you might enjoy the challenge of breaking him to boundaries.

With the light line attached, take your dog into the area where you would like him to remain, and with an "okay" release that suggests an attitude of relaxation, not horseplay, encourage him to go where he likes. Try to keep the line from tightening until he gets within a foot or so of the boundary line; then, without a word, stop him by turning or by holding solidly on the line. Give him a word of praise for his turning, and then let him know it's all right for him to return to his own interests. When he again reaches a point near a flower bed or fence, which would be a route out of the area, let your turn or jerk tell him that he's gone far enough in that direction. As common sense should tell you, concentrate on those places where the dog is most likely to exit. Don't waste time turning him away from a boundary that consists of a building or a twelve-foot wall.

Persist in this pattern of encouraging him to relax but at the same time making him conscious of the area wherein you wish him to remain. It requires a program of consistent work, free from the setbacks that would occur if the dog were given opportunity to cross the boundaries between your training periods; eventually his actions will show you that he knows where you've "drawn the line."

Now, while you watch, let him drag the line around as a reminder of the times he's been turned away from certain places. If he ventures across the boundary that you've taught him to observe, a carefully timed shot with the slingshot will show him life is better when he stays within his own area.

Next comes the critical part of this particular training. You've shown him where he should not go. Now you must supply temptation to cause him to cross the boundaries so you will have opportunity to correct him at those times when he has **the strongest possible incentive to disobey.**

Another dog or a cat on the far side of the hedge or fence should cause him to forget the boundaries and give you your opportunity. As in every case where you use the technique of maximum temptation and correction, the greatest benefits are obtained through repetition of the procedure when it seems that the dog can no longer be successfully tempted.

Each time he turns away from these strong incentives to disobedience, his quality of obedience grows stronger. Soon, even the fact that you're not around will not be sufficient to make him cross the boundaries.

There is something you can use for protection, if you feel that he might hang himself when he is dragging the line around while you're gone. Since the line at this time is a reminder and a symbol of authority more than an implement for physical correction, you can join the line to the collar with a few inches of "breakaway section" that is strong enough to drag the line but not strong enough to hold against the dog's weight or a struggle should the line catch on something.

There is almost no limit to the reliability that can be obtained by this principle of supplying the absolute maximum of temptation when you are set to correct the wrongdoer. If you have the determination, you can make "not crossing the boundary" almost a religion with your dog.

If you are short on time or ability, you

might find one of the following "mechanical aids" useful where you have a fenced area.

Here's a way you can make him feel that he's jumped from confinement into closer confinement. Fasten a line — a strong one — to his collar and tie the other end in such a way that the dog can reach only one of the routes he commonly takes over the fence. The line should be long enough to permit the dog to jump the fence without the possibility of hanging but so short that he has only a few feet of movement when he lands. You can help him to see that he's jumped into a worse situation if you are hidden out in the neighbor's yard or a nearby car. Descend on him, blister his bottom, and pitch him or drag him back over the fence.

Work the setup on all boundaries where the dog might consider jumping, adding to the surprise and unpleasant landing in every way possible. A bunch of BBs from a slingshot will contribute greatly to his reception on the wrong side of the fence.

So you've got a smarty who won't try to jump until you drive off in your car, and you don't want to give him the chance of jumping and strangling when you are gone. There is a simple and safe solution. Drive half a block in your car, switch to a friend's, and come back and park. Enough of these situations, and automobiles as well as the line will be a reminder to the dog of your omnipresence.

Even a stupid dog, if he jumps into bad situations often enough, should come to prefer the larger area of freedom and comfort of the yard he's been leaving.

When you feel it's safe to try him when you're going to be gone for a while, do so by letting him drag the line with the "breakaway section." That drag on his collar is quite a reminder of the horrible messes he's jumped into.

Some jumping-jack dogs, given to leaping over a fence or beating themselves hysterically against it, can be discouraged by a simple device consisting of a block of wood fastened to a line that is attached to the dog's collar. The line should be long enough to permit the block to drag on the ground at a point about halfway back on the dog. A hole bored through or a staple driven into the block will serve to fasten the one end of the line. The block should be of a weight to drag easily and still be heavy enough to flip against the dog with a good whack each time he jumps. In addition to supplying the whack, the block serves to throw the dog off-balance when he jumps. If, before giving up, he decided to chew free of the block, you can always substitute a length of light bronze or steel cable, obtainable at your local hardware store. Even with this unchewable, unbreakable material, there need be no danger of hanging or strangling. Simply join the cable to the collar with a breakaway section that is so close to the dog's neck that he cannot chew it.

The unbalancing, along with the whacking, usually convinces the dog that the discomfort caused by the block's dragging is not nearly so great as what he experiences when jumping, and soon he'll ease up in his attempts to clear the fence or beat it down with his lunges.

The critical time on the foregoing correction comes when it seems that the dog has quit altogether. To remove the block at this point would be to invite failure. Instead, use the principle of the "gradually diminishing reminder," which is another way of telling you to change progressively to lighter blocks until it seems that something the size of a clothespin, and finally the line itself, is an efficient discouragement to the dog's jumping.

This procedure of attaching a block can be used even more easily on a dog that crawls under or through a fence. In this case, the block should be longer than the width of the opening through which the dog crawls, with the line attached to the middle of the block so that it becomes a drag that will not follow the dog through the opening. If properly equipped, it's almost inevitable that the dog will learn his exits lead not to greater freedom but to closer confinement. If, when he finds he has tied himself into a bad situation, he tries to chew, remember to replace the first five feet of light line with the metal cable. As always, it's your responsibility to take precautions against his choking.

Whether your dog goes over, under, or through a fence, be slow to remove the line and quick to reattach it, block and all, if there should be a recurrence.

As in all types of corrective training, you must provide temptations and incentives to cause the difficult dog to disobey and consequences so discouraging that he'll wish he hadn't.

In cases where a dog is a veritable escape artist and still, because of traffic or other hazards, must be made to stay within an area, an electrically charged wire can sometimes be used to advantage, just as it is used to keep cattle, horses, and hogs confined to pastures or pens. This, of course, is the current that comes through a battery powered "fence unit," or another safe shocking device, and not the house current which would be dangerous to humans and dogs alike. Commonly, these devices have about six volts' capacity and simply startle the animal that comes in contact with the charged wire but are in no way harmful.

In most instances, even if there is a wide fence, it would be impractical and expensive to electrify it, so it is nearly always better to follow the same procedure as is recommended when the fence is wood or brick or when no fence exists.

This consists of stringing one or two strands of light, inexpensive bare wire on laths or other dry, nonconducting sticks that are stuck in the ground along the boundaries of the area where the dog is confined. You will be the judge of how high the wires should be. Naturally, the dog should not be able to walk under the bottom strand nor step over the top strand, so the difference in setups for a small dog and a large one would be great.

If any green foliage or a tree touches the wire, your circuit will be grounded out, so check it carefully before putting your dog into the area.

Even when you use the "charged wire" treatment, it's best to have your dog drag his light line as a reminder of what is right and wrong.

Possibly you've got one of those ingenious dogs who seems to know instinctively how to get past the wires without making contact. If so, try this technique: In addition to his light line, fasten a piece of wire to a ring of his collar. It should be long enough so that a few inches of the wire drag on the ground. Now, when your dog crosses the charged wire, this trailing piece will drag over it, and at the moment its end leaves the ground, your dog will get a jolting surprise.

If the wire is too long, part of it will always be grounding out. There must be a moment when the end rides over the charged wire, completely free of the ground.

Even though a six-volt circuit, such as the above, does not offer the slightest danger to the smallest baby, there are sometimes ordinances against electrified fence, so check with the authorities before using this method.

Persistence in applying one of the above techniques will convince even the most recalcitrant dog that his home area is a pretty good place to stay.

Some dogs seem more concerned with getting into the house than getting out of the yard, much to the damage of doors and even windows. You have probably heard various suggestions for correcting this screen-scratching, door-damaging activity. One of the most common suggestions is a pan of water in the face. While the waterthrowing works in some cases, I've found it to be quite ineffective in the cases of dogs that were exceptionally stubborn or spoiled.

Here is a correction that often gets results, particularly when the dog has been very receptive to obedience training. Fasten your longe line to his collar; then, with music, laughter, and other inviting sounds, make him think he's missing out on a big party. When he starts belaboring the door, rush out, grab the line, and snatch him away from the door. In the same snatching motion, put him on a long down for about twenty minutes, insisting that he hold until you come back and break him loose. If the consequences of each of these yipping, scratching demands for admission is a jerk and a long down, he will eventually conclude that life is better when he waits for an invitation.

If your dog seems completely obsessed with getting into the house regardless of rebuffs, you may save your property and your time by using the battery powered shocking device described above.

This correction has the advantage of being effective even when you're not home. With a little ingenuity, it can be adapted to any door or situation, regardless of material and the dog's footing.

For the most logical example, let's start with the simplest one: the screen door with the wooden frame, faced with a porch of cement or other grounding material. Hook your charged wire to the screen, making sure you get a good contact. Give your dog a good incentive to jump against or scratch the door. Unless he's an idiot, one experience should show him he's had it.

But what if the door has a metal frame?

By using tape, either adhesive or the new industrial variety, cover the vulnerable area of the door with cardboard. Now, onto this "insulating face," tape a strip of copper window screen, which can probably be bought as a scrap at your hardware or building materials store. Thread your charged wire into the screen, and you are ready.

And what if he scratches a wooden door?

Wood is a nonconductor, and you can stick your screen right to the surface in the dog's scratching area. You'll be ready for action as soon as you attach the charged wire.

Used consistently, one of the foregoing methods should serve to keep your dog in or out of any area you desire. But don't make the mistake of taking the early results as an indication of permanent impression and slack off too soon. Control the situation until it seems the dog has a genuine aversion to "going out" or "going in" before he is asked.

DESTRUCTIVE CHEWING

Whether a dog chews shrubs, shoes, or household treasures (and there are specialists in each field), the depredations end in one of two ways: The dog is made to stop chewing or is exiled to a situation where there is nothing to chew. The "companion" who must be exiled may sometimes be accidentally left in a chewing situation and for this reason is not nearly so satisfactory as the one who is taught to respect property.

Before going into methods of correction, you must carefully consider the possibility of a mineral deficiency in your dog's diet. Such a deficiency can cause destructive chewing that appears sheer deviltry but in reality is done to satisfy a craving for something his body lacks.

I stated in the introduction the reasons why I would leave the subject of diet to veterinarians and pet supply stores; however, the almost universal ignorance of the vitamin-happy public on the significance of basic minerals, together with the urge to chew, so often caused by mineral deficiency, makes it advisable to discuss minerals and what they do.

You know that your dog's body, like your own, is composed of minerals. Naturally, these minerals must be replenished by what you eat and drink. When the diet fails in its assignment of replenishing, the deficiency causes many body processes to fail. Assimilation and metabolism of other food substances require an adequate supply of minerals or they remain unused by the body.

A commonly observed example of how a deficiency can cause a dog to chew while seeking to satisfy a hidden hunger is found in the dog that lacks the mineral balance necessary to assimilate the sulphurbearing protein in his diet. He will actually feel a "sulphur hunger" and chew at his own hair to satisfy a perverted appetite. He'll chew other things, too, not in mischief but in his feverish seeking and so is brought to our consideration for correction. Further, since mineral deficiency causes deterioration of his nerve sheathing, he is apt to become nervous, restless, and noisy.

The foregoing points to our obligation to make certain that there is an adequate mineralization of the dog's system before punishing him for chewing.

Don't smile pityingly, explain that your dog gets everything he needs, and read the analysis off a bottle of combination vitamins and minerals. Instead, consider the experience I have had in my obedience classes. In June 1958, a commercial laboratory in California provided me with a large bulk sample of an organic mineral combination, together with the suggestion that I pass it on to the owners of those dogs in my classes whose nervous conduct or unthrifty appearance indicated a mineral deficiency.

The results were surprising to the members of the classes and of great significance. Within two weeks there was a general, favorable change in temperament and an improvement in physical condition. A good percentage of the chewing cases were corrected. In part, the surprise was due to the fact that many of the improvements were noticed in dogs whose owners had previously supplied them with "everything" in the form of vitamin-mineral combinations.

When the classes witnessed the results of mineralizing a dog's system, the question generally asked was: "What's the difference between the minerals in the combination products on the market and the ones in the sample?"

Nutritionists explain it this way: "In the first instance the minerals are not organically combined, but the minerals that produced the results were."

Organic in this case means minerals as naturally present in plant life. As the one plant grown in a medium where there is no mineral deficiency, this particular manufacturer chose sea kelp. The results of both government and private research support the company's claim that marine vegetation is the most mineral-rich plant life in the world. Doubtless this abundance of organically combined minerals from nature's storehouse is the reason that the sea kelp–based formula is able to curb nervous habits and a morbid appetite more often and to a greater degree than other products we have tested in our classes.

The humaneness and common sense of assuring that a dog has no mineral deficiencies before punishing him for acts that could be caused by such shortages needs no further justification. When this consideration has been met, you can use the following corrective techniques without inhibition.

Rather than waste time on discussions of such maneuvers as pointing to the damage a dog has done and saying, "No-no-naughty-naughty," tying the damaged article to his neck, or going through calisthenics with a folded newspaper to the rhythm of "Shame-shame-shame," let's start out with some methods that the record shows are a bit more effective. So that you might better understand the aversion, and even revulsion, caused by the first correction we'll discuss, try the following experiment.

Select a food that you like exceptionally well, cram your mouth full of it, and hold it there for awhile without chewing. In a surprisingly short time, you will experience a gagging sensation and will want to empty your mouth — not by swallowing, either. This gagging sensation in association with the taste causes a revulsion. This same principle can be used to discourage your dog from destructive chewing.

The specific technique is to select a piece of the material he has chewed (you needn't catch him in the act) and place it well back, crossways, in his mouth. Use a strip of adhesive tape to wrap the muzzle securely in front of the chewed material, so that no amount of gagging and clawing can force it from his mouth.

Perhaps you are wondering if these frantic efforts to rid himself of the material will cause the dog to scratch himself painfully. Yup. They surely will. And the person who earned the money that bought the ruined shoe or the long-awaited piece of furniture, now badly mauled, probably experienced a bit of pain when he surveyed the damage.

And if your doggie "didn't know any better," he'll know better after an hour or so of his mouth burden. When, after a long time, the tape is finally removed from his mouth (a bit of ether will remove it easily) you may find he seems to hate the sight of the object. Don't be fooled into thinking he's cured. His recent experience may be just a temporary influence. You want a permanent impression. You can work toward that permanent impression by repeating the "taping in" process the next day, even if he hasn't chewed anything in the meantime. Naturally, if he does chew before the next day, you should immediately tape the last-chewed object in his mouth.

Surveys made in obedience classes to check the effectiveness of this revulsion method show that if the handler will follow through with the taping-in for at least six days after the dog has apparently stopped chewing, 80 percent of these destructive chewers can be reformed.

Don't take a couple of days without a chewing episode as a sign that your dog doesn't need the clincher of the full six follow-up days. The stronger the "bad taste" you leave in his mouth, the more chance of a permanent impression.

Before you tell me your dog chews on something that couldn't be taped in his mouth, consider this example. If he chews on the corner of a house, and his chewing doesn't produce a splinter big enough to place in his mouth, stick a few strips of cheese boxes or light crating in those spots where he is most likely to chew. Once stuck in place with tape or a bit of glue, the boards become an inviting part of the building. It will be a "part" you can handle. With ingenuity, you can attach a convenient "part" of suitable material to anything from a sofa to a barn. *Be sure any object you might tape in his mouth is too big for him to swallow.* If he chews on an object too small to meet this precaution, provide a sufficiently large object, similarly shaped and of the same kind of material, for his sampling and correction.

For that 20 percent of the dogs that seem to feel neither revulsion nor repentance from the "taping in" but continue to destroy valuable property, more drastic measures must be taken. A wire from a shocking device (such as was previously described) can be brought into contact with the chewed object while it is in the dog's mouth. If the material is a nonconductor, it will have to be dampened so the dog will feel the tingle. *It is only in extreme cases where the dog must quit chewing "or else" that this traumatic method is recommended.* There are some dogs so destructive that no person could afford to keep them. Yet it is cruel to have them destroyed if a drastic correction can end the chewing problem.

If your dog is one who picks his "chewables" from the clothesline, your job is easy. Hang some damp clothing from a bare wire that is insulated at both ends. Connect the charged wire from a fence unit to the clothes wire, and hang some damp laundry at an inviting length. Turn on the fence unit and get out of sight so your dog will feel free to chew.

In all situations where the dog is punished, it is better to take the dog into the area where he chewed than to bring the object to him. After all, in addition to not chewing, you probably want him to stay away from the laundry, bush, or other chewed object, so let his discomfort be in those areas. When it seems like a difficult job to stop his chewing, remember that no one else can afford to keep a chewer either, so you can't write off your obligation with "free to good home."

BARKING, WHINING, HOWLING, YODELING, SCREAMING, AND WAILING

Dogs are known to emit all of the above sounds in many different keys. Unlike the chewing problem, where a loss is no concern of the neighbors, the neighbors take a heated interest in the vocal efforts of a noisy dog. Eventually, so will the law, which generally gives a choice of four procedures: (a) quiet the dog; (b) keep him in a soundproof area; (c) get rid of him; (d) move.

The fact that you realize you have such a problem makes it certain you have "reproved" the dog often enough to let him know you were against his sound effects, even though your reproving didn't quiet them, so we'll bypass the loudly clapped hands, the cup of water in his face, and the "shame-shames" and start with something more emphatic.

We'll begin with the easiest kind of vocalist to correct: the one that charges gates, fences, doors, and windows, barking furiously at familiar or imaginary people and objects. A few clusters of BBs from a good slingshot, in conjunction with the light line and plenty of temptations, will cause such a dog to use his mind rather than his mouth. But you won't make the permanent impression unless you supply dozens of opportunities for him to exercise the control he thus acquires. Make sure these opportunities don't always come at the same time of the day, else he may learn to observe the "quiet hour" and pursue his old routines at other times. With the help of the light line, it will be easy to follow the BBs with a long down to make sure he gets the most from his lesson. As was mentioned before, eliminating the senseless barking will not lessen the dog's value as a watchdog but rather, as he grows more discriminating, increase it.

The dog who vocalizes in bratty protest or lonesomeness because you're gone constitutes a different problem. If it is impractical for someone to stay with him constantly (there are owners who cater to neurosis by employing dog sitters), you'll have to heed the neighbors and the law and quiet the dog. This calls for a little ingenuity as well as a heavy hand.

Attach a line to your dog's collar, so your corrective effort doesn't turn into a footrace around the house until you reach a stalemate under the bed. This use of the line in the correction will also serve to establish it as a reminder to be quiet as the dog drags it around when you're not present. Next, equip yourself with a man's leather belt or a strap heavy enough to give your particular dog a good tanning. Yup — we're going to strike him. Real hard. *Remember, you're dealing with a dog who knows he should be quiet and neighbors who have legal rights to see that he does.*

Now leave, and let your fading footsteps tell the dog of your going. When you've walked to a point where he'll think you're gone but where you could hear any noises he might make, stop and listen. If you find a comfortable waiting place on a nearby porch, be careful not to talk or laugh. Tests show a dog's hearing to be many times as sharp as yours.

When the noise comes, instead of trying to sneak up to the door so you can barge in while he's still barking, which is generally impossible, respond to his first sound with an emphatic bellow of "out," and keep on bellowing as you charge back to his area. Thunder through the door or gate, snatch up the belt that you've conveniently placed, and descend on him. He'll have no chance to dodge if you grab the line and reel him in until his front feet are raised off the floor or, if he's a big dog, until you've snubbed him up with a hitch on something. While he's held in close, lay the strap vigorously against his thighs. Keep pouring it on him until he thinks it's the bitter end. A real whaling now may cut down somewhat on the number of repeat performances that will be necessary. When you're finished and the dog is convinced that he is, put him on a long down to think things over while you catch your breath. After fifteen or twenty minutes, release him from the stay and leave the area again.

So that you won't feel remorseful, reflect on the truth that a great percentage of the barkers who are given away to "good homes" end up in the kindly black box with the sweet smell. Personally, I've always felt that it's even better to spank children, even if they "cry out," than to "put them to sleep."

You might have a long wait on that comfortable porch before your dog starts broadcasting again. When he does, let your long range bellow tie the consequent correction to his first sound and repeat the spanking, if anything emphasizing it a bit more.

It might be necessary to spend a Saturday or another day off so that you'll have time to follow through sufficiently. When you have a full day, you will be able to convince him each yelp will have a bad consequence, and the consistency will make your job easier. If he gets away with his concert part of the time, he'll be apt to gamble on your inconsistency.

After a half-dozen corrections, "the reason and the correction" will be tied in close enough association so that you can move in on him without the preliminary bellowing of "out." From then on, it's just a case of laying for the dog and supplying enough bad consequences of his noise so he'll no longer feel like gambling.

Occasionally, there is a dog who seems to sense that you're hiding nearby and will utter no sound. He also seems to sense when you have really gone away, at least according to the neighbors. Maybe his sensing actually amounts to close observation. He could be watching and listening for the signs of your actual going.

Make a convincing operation of leaving, even if it requires changing clothes and being unusually noisy as you slam the doors on the family car and drive away. Arrange with a friend to trade cars a block or two from your house so you can come back and park within earshot without a single familiar sound to tell the dog you've returned. A few of these car changes are generally enough to fool the most alert dog.

Whether your dog believes you are gone anytime you step out of the house or requires the production of changing clothes and driving off, keep working until even your neighbors admit the dog has reformed. If there has been a long history of barking and whining, it sometimes requires a lot of work to make a dog be quiet when you're not around, so give the above method an honest try before you presume your dog requires a more severe correction.

Finally, if your dog is uninfluenced by the punishment and the reminder of the dragging line, you may be able to silence him with the mystery of a tingle from a properly used electric fence unit, such as has already been described.

Danger! If it's used as a shortcut gimmick by a handler who is lazy or less intelligent than his dog, electricity can cause great nervousness in an animal. The current cult of "stock-prod-happy" incompetents who can't meet a dog on even intellectual terms has caused nervousness in many dogs that could have been effectively corrected with a different method. *The use of electricity is recommended only when the spanking method fails to quiet a dog that must be quieted — or else.*

As an example, if your dog does his noise

making in the yard, fasten one end of a bright shiny chain to a tree limb with a piece of rope so that the chain doesn't come into contact with the tree or other conducting surfaces. As to length, when the other end is fastened to your dog's collar, he should be able to move around in a considerable radius with the chain's being free of the ground nearly all of the time. The area of movement will be quite great if the chain is tied at least six feet above the ground.

To the upper end of the chain fasten the charged wire from a six-volt shocking device. The chain will serve to conduct the electricity to the collar. Since your dog might panic, it is recommended that he be secured to the chain with a leather collar as well as the metal collar that will conduct the current.

The situation should be set up so that the current can be flicked on and off without the dog's being aware that anyone is around. If you have to drive off in the car before your dog will make a sound, hide someone in the house to operate the switch for you. Though hidden, it is very important that the person be able to see the dog.

Instruct your helper carefully. When the noise begins, he should flick the switch on until the dog gets a jolt, and then flick it back off. Most of the time this first tingle will be followed by a startled yelp and silence. There should be no more current turned on until the dog's noise begins again.

However, don't take the sounds of panic as intentional barking. Let the dog fight the panic out with the chain until he settles down. Protected as he is by the leather collar, the dog is not apt to injure himself with frantic jerking and, finding the chain unyielding, will eventually settle down. If and when the bratty noises recur, they should be met with another jolt. If there is no discomfort when the dog is not barking, the dog will be apt to remember just what he did to cause the shocking experience to be repeated. Three or four experiences should be enough to convince your dog that you can outmaneuver him whether you're home or gone.

In the house, the mechanics of the correction are a bit more complex. If you lack the technical skill, get assistance from someone who could rig a proper circuit to use the above principles in the inside situation. Undoubtedly there is someone in your neighborhood who can check your situation and figure the set-up out for you.

Once more, *use the "tingle" only if absolutely necessary and then very carefully.*

BITING

The small percentage of dogs that bite people is monumental proof that the dog is the most benign, forgiving creature on earth.

However, embarrassment, danger, liability, and the law demand that "something" be done about the few dogs who do bite. If you have a shred of conscience, you'll find it tough to unreservedly accept that "something" as putting the dog to sleep, particularly since there is a possibility that stupid handling may have implanted and cultivated the dog's biting career.

Because the motivations that make dogs bite are varied, it follows that the corrections must also differ in type and application. We had best take each example in close association with the specific correction recommended.

THE PROTEST BITER

As was necessary, we dealt exhaustively with the "protest biter" when we started to handle the dog during the early obedience exercises. One thing might be added: Because the reasonable protest could be in peculiar situations where the dog would attempt to avoid correction, it is wise to give him a lot of experience with a line hanging from his collar. With the line to remind him that he can't take his bite and escape unpunished, the dog will form new habits. Let him drag a short line until he no longer protests the reasonable actions of people who mean no harm and possibly are trying to help him.

THE OVERLY POSSESSIVE DOG

This extremist is more "screwball" than guard dog. Even after a person has been properly admitted to a house or room, this neurotic lies hoping they'll walk toward his fetish, which is often a silly toy, so he can justify a bite. This possession may be an area as well as an object. A corner, the "cave" beneath a table, and a closet are good examples.

With a wholesome assertion of rights and without the slightest appearance of teasing, set up some training situations. Use a helper who is able to cooperate intelligently. For the protection of the helper and yourself, as well as a necessary facility, in the beginning have a piece of line as heavy as your longe line attached to the dog's collar. Put him on a stay, and make him hold it while your helper moves around in the "sacred area."

If the dog moves aggressively, make the correction as explained earlier, and then put him back into position. He can't very well stay and charge at the same time and will eventually come to associate the imagined intrusion with the necessity of restraint. This is a gradual process but nearly always effective. It seems that the dog who learns not to break a stay in order to bite readily learns to restrain his aggressiveness when at liberty in the same situations. Work on it. Your chances of winning a complete victory are excellent.

THE CHASE-HAPPY BITER

This type of dog, with the tremendous drive he expresses in chasing and biting at people who are running, skating, or riding such things as bikes, scooters, motorcycles, and horses, needs basic obedience — but plenty. After you've added to his restraint and conscience by having him hold lots of stays while exposed to the temptations, you can stimulate him with the same distractions without his being told to stay. What you do with the stays is to make him think well before charging anything.

Be certain of two things: first, that he is equipped with a good strong line; second, that if he moves one inch aggressively, he'll wish he hadn't. Remember, you are liable if his charge, with or without a bite, should cause someone to fall and be injured. So grab the line and give him about five minutes of the hardest tanning you can administer. Use a belt heavy enough to make him really feel your efforts. Sometimes the long duration of a spanking is a big factor in making an indelible impression. *Since you're dealing with a dog that could cause the death or serious injury of a person, let there be no compassionate trembling before the necessity of stern measures.*

Truthfully, it might be well to explain your situation to the police so they'll know you'll have to make a better citizen of your dog, even if you have to do it the hard way; then they'll be prepared to answer any protest from kind folks who would rather have your dog put to sleep than punished.

When, after a few days' work, it seems that nothing can get your dog to ignore you and the line nor react to the distractions, you may be sure of one thing. You're well started — that's all.

The successive steps that make the permanent impression are well demonstrated by the example of a dog I know in Riverside, California. This Boxer, one of the very few of her breed who seem to want to chase bicycles, was obsessed with the two-wheeled monsters. When finally, by means of the line and effective use of the slingshot, she appeared ready to turn away from instead of toward bikes, observers felt that she would backslide when no one was around. They didn't reckon with the determination of the mistress. Literally, the woman put a boy on the payroll to ride back and forth in front of the house. When the dog lost all interest in bikes, the owner restored it by having the boy drag a burlap sack of tin cans behind him. This swishing, clattering bicycle was much more tempting than any straight, production-line model, and when the inevitability of punishment, fortified by hundreds of times of wearisome exposure, finally caused an allergy to the ultra-attractive model, the feeling became the dog's permanent attitude toward all bikes. It was the hundreds of chances to say "No, I won't" that actually "brainwashed" the dog.

So follow the example. When the line and punishment have caused your dog to say "no," make the attitude permanent by giving him hundreds of opportunities to repeat the "no."

THE SNEAK BITER

This dog is the type who lurks in his lair behind a bush or under the table, ready to glide out and nip a human whom his imagination has changed to a tiger. Even those indulgent folks who thought the "stalking game" was quite cute during their dog's puppyhood grow tired of the tiger role and wish to stop the game. And it is generally a game, more than a sign of viciousness, and as a rule, not too difficult to stop.

After attaching the longe line to your dog's collar, place him on a down-stay in the lair where he most likes to lurk, and have a number of people go by at various rates of speed but with no appearance of teasing. Make him hold for at least a half hour. The reason? There are three: First, he's developing restraint in the exact situation where he needs it. Second, the continued exercising of the restraint makes the situation a bit boring and distasteful. And third, by associating the boredom with the situation where he has played his "game," he comes to regard the process more and more as a direct punishment of his sneak attacks. Give it a good try. Then you will know you've dealt fairly with your dog; if he requires more emphatic discouragement, you can conscientiously give him a good tanning for each attempt to bite. When he no longer rises to the bait of a person walking by, continue to leave the line on while you give him many opportunities to say, "No, I won't." As in all your training, find ways to show your appreciation when he makes the right decisions.

HOUSEBREAKING

For most dog owners, housebreaking begins with a puppy. Because he eats one or two more meals a day than a grown dog, the puppy requires more frequent opportunities to relieve himself. This fact is often mentioned and too often forgotten. Carefully observe your pup's digestive cycle. Try to work out a regular schedule of feeding that will permit you to take the pup out about the time he generally needs an airing, and you'll be taking advantage of the pup's instincts for cleanliness. The less your carelessness forces him to violate his precepts of cleanliness, the more control he will develop.

The second consideration in the housebreaking of a puppy is the practice of close confinement when he's out of your sight. Whenever possible, keep him in view when he's in the house, so you'll see the signs of his need and be able to take him outdoors.

A puppy collar with a short piece of line dragging from it is one of the best assurances that, feeling guilty if he starts to commit an error, he won't try to run from you and complicate matters in more ways than one. The line also serves to remind him of his responsibilities.

When you must be out of sight of the pup, don't leave him to his own devices before he is housebroken. Confine him in a dog crate of the proper size so that he would be soiling the area in which he is held. Dogs as a rule don't like to be in close proximity to the mess they make and will restrain themselves until they are let out. Since it prepares the pup for later traveling and confinement when ill, the crate is by far the best way to confine a dog. However, if you cannot buy or make a crate, tie him on a short chain on a floor that is nonabsorbent. Absorbent surfaces are pretty much an invitation for a pup to relieve himself. That's why he will seek out and use the newspapers intended for the purpose and will leave the linoleum to go to an inviting rug. So keep him confined during those moments when you are not observing him. Close observation and few opportunities for messing will get the job done much sooner than newspapers and punishment.

If your dog is a bit more dirty than the average or your schedule won't permit close observation, you may have to use papers. Use a stack an eighth of an inch thick. Spread them out in an area where the dog will be forced to take his choice between the papers and the nonabsorbent area around them. Do not give him the run of the house so he will have his choice between the papers and a softer, more inviting area, such as a rug. The closer the papers are placed to a door leading to the outside, the better. Drop a few of these soiled stacks of paper in a section of the yard where you would like your dog to relieve himself. Then, when you are going to be in the room to observe him, see that no papers are on the floor, and when he appears to be seeking them for his purpose, take him out and place him in close proximity to the soiled papers. Tie him or in some other way keep him in the area until, encouraged by the smell and his own need, he relieves himself. Show your pleasure at his good manners and take him back into the house.

Soon he'll know that his signs of agitation, as he seeks the papers, will get a response from you. A bit of recognition, such as "Want out, boy?" or "Let's go," will help set the procedure of letting you know. Once you get him started in the right behavior pattern, his reliability will grow rapidly.

Occasionally, there is a pup who seems determined to relieve himself inside the house, regardless of how often he has the opportunity to go outside. This dog may require punishment. Make certain he is equipped with a collar and piece of line so he can't avoid correction.

When you discover a mess, move in fast, take him to the place of his error, and hold his head close enough so that he associates his error with the punishment. Punish him by spanking him with a light strap or switch. Either one is better than a folded newspaper.

It is important to your future relationship that you do not rush at him and start swinging before you get hold of him.

When he's been spanked, take him outside. Chances are, if you are careful in your feeding and close observation, you will not have to do much punishing. Be consistent in your handling. To have a pup almost housebroken and then force him to commit an error by not providing an opportunity to go outside is very unfair. Careful planning will make your job easier.

The same general techniques of housebreaking apply to grown dogs that are inexperienced in the house.

For the grown dog who was reliable in the house and then backslides, the method of correction differs somewhat. In this group of "backsliders" we have the "revenge piddler." This dog protests being alone by messing on the floor and often in the middle of a bed.

The first step of correction is to confine the dog closely in a part of the house when you go away, so that he is constantly reminded of his obligation. The fact that he once was reliable in the house is proof that the dog knows right from wrong, and it leaves you no other course than to punish him sufficiently to convince him that the satisfaction of his wrongdoing is not worth the consequences. If the punishment is not severe enough, some of these "backsliders" will think they're winning and will continue to mess in the house. An indelible impression can sometimes be made by giving the dog a hard spanking of long duration, then leaving him tied by the mess he's made so you can come back at twenty-minute intervals and punish him again for the same thing. In most cases, the dog that deliberately does this disagreeable thing cannot be made reliable by the light spanking that some owners seem to think is adequate punishment. It will be better for your dog, as well as the house, if you really pour it on him.

Some of the new "breaking scents" on the market can aid in your housebreaking program. One type discourages the dog from even visiting an area. Another encourages him to relieve himself in the area where it is sprinkled. Your pet shop should be able to supply further information on the brands available in your district.

Be fair to your dog in what and when you feed him and be consistent in your efforts to housebreak him, and you'll soon accomplish the job.

THE DOG FIGHTING PROBLEM

The recommendation, contained in the introduction of this book, that all of the contents be read before the training of the dog is begun, is urgently advocated, particularly in the case of the fighting dog. Often dogs that are bluffs or inexperienced will become socially well adjusted from the benefits of obedience training, with a bit of emphasis on setting up problems and using the throw-chain.

However, if your dog is uninfluenced by the ordinary approach to the problem, your concern for his safety and welfare as well as your own doesn't leave any course but to take the necessary steps to break him from fighting. Two dogs can do so much damage to each other or to humans who might be bitten in trying to separate them that even the most emotionally unstable person can hardly protest any strong measure necessary to make a fighter into a peaceful citizen.

One method has been proven so far superior to others that there is hardly any reason to discuss other techniques. It is a method that I have used hundreds of times in my obedience classes on fighting dogs, many of which had been sent to me as a "last resort" by police departments and humane organizations.

Objectively, here is how a qualified trainer would proceed. A helper, well coordinated and intelligent, holds another dog that the fighter would likely challenge about fifty feet away from the dog to be corrected. A hose, such as described for dealing with a biter, is held out of sight in the trainer's right hand. The leash is wound up short around the left hand.

Without a word from the handler, the fighting dog is moved directly toward the other dog until he is close enough to be tempted to try a lunge. At the first growl or aggressive move the hose is brought down across the middle of his muzzle. If the correction is forceful enough, it is certain the thoughts of fighting will be removed from the dog's mind for at least a few moments. Now comes the important part. The fighting dog is not held back but actually pulled toward the dog that he tried to attack. This strange attitude, where the handler confronts him with an opportunity instead of restraining him, is the principle that really makes the correction pay off. Even though the dog turns his head — and most do after one correction — he is pressured toward the other dog over and over until it seems he has formed such an aversion that he does not want to see the other animal.

Consistent action on the part of the trainer tells the dog that each time he shows aggressive intent or growls at another dog, he will get the correction on the muzzle and then be pulled up close for his "opportunities." When he realizes that the full consequence is the unvarying result of his attempts to fight, he will begin to form his own aversions to combat.

No qualified trainer would ever dream of threatening the dog with the hose, to the accompaniment of such asinine drivel as, "You'd better not, or you'll get it." A trainer wants a dog to mind when he's not around to threaten. It can be stated very simply: The dog should receive the correction each and every time he makes the slightest aggressive move.

As was advised in the other two situations where severe correction has been proven the proper course to follow, if there is any doubt as to your ability to duplicate the procedure of a competent trainer and make a safe and effective correction, do not attempt it. Nevertheless, the author has a moral obligation to inform the owners of the confirmed fighters that there is a correction that might convert their dogs from the dangerous practice of fighting and possibly save them from being destroyed as incorrigibles.

In connection with the handling of fighters,

you will be interested in reading the affidavit in the front of the book. It is certainly proof that to give up too soon on the correction of a fighter cannot be called kindness.

JUMPING ON PEOPLE

By now you know that a dog's good behavior habits around his master and others can generally be established by the proper use of obedience. This is especially true in the case where a dog jumps on a person. Obedience will also curb a dog's exuberance and make him feel less inclined to jump.

If your dog is one of those rare ones who continues to jump on folks, even though obedience has been used intelligently and consistently, you'll have to follow up with other methods.

The easiest situation is where your dog jumps on you. Instead of trying to step on his back toes (which can be very difficult in the case of a big or agile dog), raise your knee sharply upward so he meets it as he jumps against you. If your action was emphatic enough, he should bounce off, quite surprised. If you are soft or poorly timed in your motions, he'll think he's discovered a delightful new game and be sure to jump on you all the more. Follow through on the knee thrust each time he jumps on you. When he starts to get reluctant, pat your chest, jump up and down, and in other ways make him forget his suspicions and venture a jump. The fact that the knee was ready will make his reluctance more permanent than if the matter had been dropped when he first grew suspicious. It would be unfair if you were to call his name when you're tempting him, but there is nothing unfair about your bouncing excitedly up and down. He'll soon get fed up with the game the way you play it.

The job of teaching him not to jump on others is a bit more difficult. Many people are loath to correct someone else's dog emphatically, and their efforts are no better than nothing at all. But you probably can find at least four or five well-coordinated friends who can use a knee effectively. Arrange to have at least two or three arrive as company, one after the other, and use the correction. The next day, invite one or two others over for the same purpose. This consolidated effort seems to be much more effective than the occasional correction interspersed with several opportunities to jump without the bad consequences. Make sure that all members of the family are consistent in thwarting the dog's jumping at all times. It is most cruel for a person to encourage a dog to jump on him when he is dressed in old clothes and then correct him because the dog jumps on him when he is dressed to go out. It is very important to keep the percentage of times he is corrected considerably greater than the number of times he is able to jump unscathed. Be alert to use his obedience training in ways that will discourage the jumping. Remember, no dog can hold a sit-stay and jump on someone at the same time.

Another effective way of correcting the dog that jumps on people other than his master is to make sure the throw-chain is in your hand and you are standing in good position to use it every time he has an opportunity to jump. Naturally, you'll follow the procedure of having a great many people approach invitingly — never teasingly — so that there will be many opportunities to use the chain. This method is especially good for correcting a dog that jumps on children too small to cooperate by using the knee technique. Often it is a combination of all the methods that stops this bad habit.

OVEREXUBERANCE

There is one cure for overexuberance, and it is a sure cure. First, thoroughly obedience train your dog. Seek out situations that will stimulate his exuberance, and practice your controls at the highest point of excitement. This will invariably develop his capacity for restraint and make him take the distracting situation as a cue to be calm. A determined handler can always correct this problem.

HOLE DIGGING

After a dog has dug a few ruinous holes in a lawn or flower bed, it is almost certain his master has shown him he disapproves, and the dog has not been particularly impressed by the disapproval. Generally, the first action of the master is to focus the dog's attention on the hole that's been dug and spank him. Sometimes this procedure accomplishes the purpose, but there are other ways that seem more effective.

If you come home and find your dog has dug a hole, fill the hole to its brim with water. With the training collar and leash, bring the dog to the hole and shove his nose into the water; hold him there until he is sure he's drowning. If your dog is of any size, you may get all of the action of a cowboy bull-dogging a steer. Stay with it. I've had elderly ladies who'd had their fill of ruined flower beds dunk some mighty big dogs. A great many dogs will associate this horrible experience with the hole they dug. However, to make sure of a permanent impression, fill the hole with water and repeat the experience the next day, whether the dog digs any more or not. On the third day, let him watch you dig a hole and prepare it for a dunking. Class surveys have shown that more than 70 percent of the dogs who experience this correction for as many as six consecutive days swear off hole digging. If the master takes the first sign of repentance as a permanent change and stops the dunking after only a couple of days, failure is generally the result.

Another correction found to be very effective and easier to administer is the policy of putting a screw-in stake in the ground adjacent to the hole, tying the dog to it on about two feet of chain, and leaving him to meditate for an hour or so. If this is the inevitable result of each excavation, the dog will eventually turn his energy to other channels.

It is not necessary to "catch the dog in the act" in any of the above instances of correction. Be consistent in your corrections and your dog will come to find the smell of freshly dug earth quite repugnant.

POISON PROOFING

The vile names that his deeds call forth are probably taken as a compliment by the twisted mind of a dog poisoner. Convictions seem altogether too few and the sentences for the crime too light. The only source of satisfaction for a dog owner lies in poison-proofing his dog.

Because poison is so often fatal, it is unwise to risk a dog's life to anything less than the most effective method of protecting a dog. Reminding you that it's your dog's life you're betting on them, we'll dispense with such superficialities as having a stranger hand the dog some food filled with a bad tasting center, carefully placed and baited traps, or the master's babbling of "no, no, no" as his dog seems about to eat food that is offered or found.

One method of poison proofing far excels any other. It is also the easiest to use. If you will follow through by applying it in every type of situation where your dog would be vulnerable to a poisoner, you will be providing your dog with certain protection.

The materials you'll need are a low-priced, battery-operated fence charger and enough light, insulated wire to run from where you will conceal the unit to the different areas where you want to proof your dog against eating food. Regardless of the spots where you set the charger, the dog shouldn't see it or hear it and be warned that something strange is taking place. Both the fence charger and suitable wire can be obtained at a hardware store for a price that is small to one who feels the need to protect his dog.

At a place where the dog is particularly vulnerable to a poisoner, we'll make our first setup in your yard. Lock your dog up so he cannot watch. Set the fence unit in a place of concealment, attach the ground wire to a pipe or a rod in the ground and the live wire to the place designated. Run the other end of the charged wire to the spot where you feel someone might be likely to toss a bit of poisoned food. Bare half an inch or so of the end of this wire. On this bare end, stick a bit of meat or other moist food that would appeal to your dog. Starting an inch back from the food, bend a couple of angles in the wire so that the bare part and the food will be held free of contact with the ground. Turn on the fence charger. Let the dog out into the yard.

Eventually your dog will find the food. If you are watching at his moment of discovery, you'll see that his first sniff will be met with a fat spark. He'll not be apt to try the second sniff, but keep some bait on the hot wire for at least two days. Then change the setup to another part of the yard. If possible, conceal the wire in heavy grass or cover it with dirt, allowing the tip to protrude to hold the tidbit free of the ground. This will make the food appear just as though it were tossed over the fence.

When your dog has had opportunity to develop resistance to food found in all areas where a poisoner might toss it, you can supply experience that will make him form an equal aversion to any food offered by hand. You'll need an outsider to help you. (Possibly you can exchange services with another dog lover who might want to protect his pet.) As with the case of something being found on the ground, run the bare tip of the live wire into the tidbit. Now, however, it is offered in the person's hand, insulated from his skin by a rubber glove or a bit of cardboard, plastic, or other nonconductive material. Change situations and strangers until you feel that, in or out of the house, no one could coax your dog to eat anything he might offer.

With sufficient follow-through in applying the above method, you can be sure your dog will decline any food that might be found or offered and eat only out of his own dish. This resistance should make him quite poison-proof.

STEALING

Canine kleptomania is entirely different from the spirit in which a dog takes an object to use as a plaything. Often one of these "lightfingered" dogs will take something that strikes his fancy — from a figurine to pruning shears — and hide it. And a puzzled neighbor may be hospitably received with a wagging rear and smiling eyes as he eases close to the dog's home porch for a closer look at a rake that resembles the one he's been missing.

Because the dog's taste and range are so varied, it is sometimes difficult to "hotwire" or "mousetrap" enough different objects to make him think that crime doesn't pay. However, difficult though it is, the procedure of "booby-trapping" tempting and strategically placed items is still the best way of starting to correct the stealing fault in a dog. This "booby-trapping" will make him more thoughtful in his choosing, but it's certain that he'll be able to steal some objects that have not been planted. It is also certain that you'll discover some of his loot. Whether you discover these stolen articles five minutes or five weeks after they disappeared, apply the "revulsion principle" of taping them in his mouth in the manner described in the instructions for dealing with chewing. Some of the articles will be of such nature as to make the task difficult, but for the most part the principle can be applied to things that a dog can pick up and steal.

Again, before starting, carefully review the instructions for taping objects in a dog's mouth (given in the section on chewing) and the methods of using a fence charger (given in the section on poison-proofing). Used consistently in combination, they will convince your dog that crime doesn't pay.

There are times when a dog trainer will "luck into" a technique of surprising value in preventing a dog from forming a specific bad habit. This happened to me when I was preparing a German Shepherd pup for a very long trip where he would be confined in my car while traveling and in a motel room at night, which in all cases could give a bored pup an opportunity to chew tempting articles. A device I used discouraged him from even touching forbidden things. It's easy to make.

Get a big coffee can of at least a two- or three-pound size, and punch a hole in it near the rim so you can pass a string through it to make a tie. Collect about ten cat food cans and wash them out thoroughly so there is no residual odor to appeal to a curious dog.

Decide where you will set the coffee can about five feet above the floor in a room with a bare wood or linoleum floor, no rugs. Generally, a spot on top of a refrigerator is about the right height.

Using the hole in the rim of the can, tie a string or fishing line about two feet longer than is needed to run down to the floor.

Put the little cat food cans in the big can and move it to where it overlaps the edge of the surface on which it stands so a slight tug on the string would tip it over the edge.

Now, to the bottom end of the string, tie a glove, a sock, or other tempting article you want to train your dog to avoid.

Close the door or tie the dog off near the temptation. If he grasps the temptation, there will be quite a crash as the big can hits the floor, and then the small cans will clatter and roll in all directions, with the never-ending sound of coins rolling down a church aisle. Apparently, the sound of rolling cans that reinforces the startling crash is important to influencing the dog.

Continue the setups, using a variety of objects and materials to which the dog will be exposed and which you want him to avoid touching.

Another value of this device is that it serves to inform you of a dog's transgression, even if you are in a far part of the house, so you can follow up with your coordinated show of disapproval.

I have received a lot of feedback on the above process that indicates it is equally effective for puppies and adult dogs.

THE PREDATOR

The law and the public have little sympathy for a predatory dog. In most areas, on the slightest evidence that a dog is even harassing domestic animals, a farmer may, with impunity, kill the dog. In some instances this attitude and legality may be justified; in other cases they are abused. Certainly, both possibilities, together with consideration for the animals a dog attacks, point to the need for correction. Confinement alone is not the answer. Dogs do get out.

The predatory fault is so serious that it calls for the most effective correction. Therefore, we'll merely mention the more commonly known methods, such as punishing a dog when "caught in the act"; tying the dead fowl or animal around the dog's neck until time and decay make him quite tired of the burden and its smell; beating him with the thing he's killed; and similar procedures. We'll get right to a method that has proven almost infallible. The dog who preys on chickens makes a good example with which to demonstrate principles that can be applied to all domestic animals and poultry.

Obtain a cull chicken from a poultryman or farmer. Borrow or buy an electric fence unit such as previously described in this chapter.

Begin by placing a piece of cardboard about two feet square in a suitable place for your dog to spot a chicken. Push a sharp stick down through its center so you will have a stake a few inches high on which to anchor the bird. Fasten a few coils of the fence charger's live wire to one of the chicken's legs, tie the legs together, and seat him as comfortably as possible in the middle of the cardboard. Secure his legs to the stake so his wingbeats can't move him from the insulating surface of the cardboard.

Experts tell me that it takes a lot of electricity to even make a chicken tingle, so feel no compunctions when you turn on the six-volt charger. Let your dog come into the area; then hurry to conceal yourself so that he won't be the least bit influenced by your presence.

Even if you should miss the sight of his contact with the chicken, you'll hear the sound effects, and odds are that your astounded dog will drown out the chicken. One thing is certain — he won't be chewing on the chicken when you get back to the area. If he hasn't retreated as far as possible, he'll have pulled well back to where he can risk a safe and bewildered look.

This first experience means you're well started. I repeat, well started — next comes the longer and more important part of the correction.

If you have a small pen or can make one about six feet square, place your cardboard, chicken, and fence charger setup in the middle of it. Turn on the current. Lock your dog in the pen with the chicken. He was a dog that always liked an opportunity to grab a chicken; now, suddenly, life is just one big, overflowing, ever-present opportunity to do just that. And if he decides to say "no," there will be hours and hours of time to repeat the "no," because the greater part of each day for at least a week should provide this opportunity to grab a chicken or refuse to do so. It is the process of this "mental laundromat," more than the initial shock, that cleanses a dog's mind of naughty thoughts toward his fellow creatures.

If it is impossible to provide the "companionette quarters" of a small pen for the dog and the object of his avowed goodwill, you can tie the dog on a five-foot chain and place the chicken setup well within the radius of his reach.

As was said before, this example of correcting the chicken-killing dog demonstrates a method that can be used to correct dogs that prey on all domestic animals and poultry. In the case of cats, rabbits, and other animals that might be hard to tie down, you can easily place the creature in a very small cage with such fine wire and large mesh that it seems openly exposed to the dog.

You can set the cage on cardboard and run your live wire to the wire on the cage. Make sure that all of the cage wire is linked together so none of it will fail to be electrified.

Your dog will feel very close to the animal in the cage. After he's had his surprise, follow through by putting him and his newfound buddy in the small pen or by tying him so that he is constantly in grabbing distance of the other animal. As in the case of the dog that kills chickens, he needs these hours of opportunity to say "no."

Either by figuring a way to keep him away from the wires of the small cage that holds him or by arranging to turn the current off and on, provide a means of protecting the animal from long periods of shock. Slight jolts that would go unnoticed by a bird would cause discomfort to an animal. Your dog, of course, brings his discomfort down on himself.

After a week during which he's had at least forty or fifty hours of opportunity, "no" will become a new way of life.

Some dogs are so predatory by nature that they will require more than the average effort. Watch your dog's attitude carefully, and be thorough in your application of the correction. Remember the law and the fact that one of the lives you save may be your dog's.

CARSICKNESS

Since continued carsickness is almost always in part due to a mental condition caused by an early unpleasant experience, it follows that a change of attitude is basic to correction of this inconvenient and messy situation. The best way to bring about this change of attitude, along with a physical accustoming, is by very short, pleasant trips over a straight road and while the dog has an empty stomach.

Literally, each ride should end before the dog has time to get sick, even if it means limiting the beginning experiences to a block in distance.

Together with a progressive increase in distance, there should be a happy conclusion to the trip, such as a walk, some play, or another bit of enjoyment that will "backwash" into the experience in a way that will make the dog regard cars more favorably.

As an aid to making these early experiences as pleasant as possible, you can procure some anti-carsickness pills from your veterinarian.

However, the progressively lengthening rides are still the fundamental part of making your dog a good traveler.

THREE PHONY PHOBIAS

I was once invited to be a guest speaker at a meeting for a dog club in Arizona. At the time, there were two flights each day from the airport near my home in California to Phoenix, one in the morning and one at night. This meant I had to land in Phoenix close to noon and wait several hours for the club meeting. The club officer who met me at the airport introduced himself as Bob and suggested it was time for lunch. We ate a leisurely meal and lingered in the cool restaurant and, of course, talked about dogs.

I found the tall, likeable Bob to be very knowledgeable about dog matters in general and about German Shepherd dogs, his breed, in particular. It was when we zeroed in on "shy dogs" that we shared a grin. Bob led off with an account of a beautifully conformed Shepherd bitch that withdrew behind her handler when approached by a judge.

"I'm supposed to meet her in the park in about a half-hour so I can help her," he said with a glance at his watch. "Would you like to come along? Or do you want to stay at my house where it's cool?"

"I'll go with you," I told him.

The woman with her Shepherd pulled into the park just ahead of us. She hurried off the hot pavement and onto the nearby grass. Bob directed her to where a row of trees made a long strip of shade.

While Bob introduced us, the Shepherd moved up to me and sniffed my hand.

"Set her up," Bob said.

The woman took a couple of steps that walked the bitch into a perfect stance that showed off her beautiful structure, said, "Jenny, stay," and took a handler's position at Jenny's right side.

Bob, with his left hand hanging down so Jenny could sniff it, stepped closer with the manner of a judge.

Jenny backed up fast and curled her body around the woman's leg and peered at Bob. Her pupils were not dilated and she showed no sign of panic or fear-biting as Bob moved in on her.

As Jenny moved against her leg, the woman cooed in soft, consoling tones. Her left hand went down and gently stroked the pretty head.

"Set her up again," Bob told the woman.

Again, Jenny walked into the classical Shepherd stance, and again Bob moved in, and Jenny backed around the woman's leg and pressed tightly against her. But the significant moves were not Jenny's. In coordination with Jenny's actions, the woman began to coo and stroke until Bob backed away. I could tell she was wondering why Bob didn't move in and go over to Jenny.

"How long have you been doing that?" Bob asked.

"Doing what?" she wanted to know.

"Sweet-talking and stroking when she acts like a craven coward. You let her break the stand-stay. Set her up again, but this time get set to move fast, because this time when Jenny backs off, I want you to lunge forward and jerk her back to where she was told to stay. Don't care if she lands with her legs crossed and a hump in her back. And don't reassure her and stroke her. Your response to her act has been making her think you approve of what she does when she breaks a stand-stay. When you get her holding a stay while someone approaches, you can start back on making her look good. Let her know she must hold the stay for anyone who comes."

The expression on Jenny's face was interesting as the correction ended with her nose almost against Bob's leg and in contact with his hand. She had experienced a rude awakening, but she was in no way confused. After all, she had been left on a stay, and to let a dog believe that unqualified fear can be an acceptable excuse is to increase its phony shyness.

Bob, Jenny, and her mistress practiced the exercise a few more times. The woman said she understood her mistake, and she would turn away from the "experts" who advised a program of pleasant familiarizing.

Her follow-through was good, and another person from Arizona told me, a few months later, that Jenny had subsequently earned both her conformation championship and an obedience title.

I often recall the example of Jenny's return to reality and, with it, other examples of induced shyness that were corrected by using an obedience exercise to extinguish a phobia. The wider and more solid the spectrum of obedience was, the more easily the problem could be handled.

Perhaps the most memorable was a Pug that was going through one of my Open classes and supposedly had a real problem with man-shyness. The dog's mistress had done a good job on force-breaking him to retrieve but had not been able to stabilize him to the approach of a man. I had seen the dog retrieve his dumbbell under some varied conditions around animals and other distractions, so she was well prepared to start on her problem.

I placed three men from the class so that two of them faced each other from a distance of a few feet and the third man to face the space between them from about that same distance, so that the three men formed a pocket. I had the woman place the Pug in a direction that would take it between the men, she moved in to make a correction that sent him scrambling for the dumbbell.

On the second setup, the Pug moved in quickly and grabbed the dumbbell. It was easy to see that the strength of his responsibility was greater than the phony fear of the men.

She gave the little dog lots of enthusiastic praise and worked him a few more times. I instructed her to work the Pug in situations that would involve the presence of men and around other phobic threats that the dog might try to use as an excuse for not retrieving.

Within a couple of weeks, the Pug had turned his attention from imagined threats to the responsibility to retrieve and the praise he would get for doing so. Soon, under all conditions, he accepted men as a part of a normal situation.

The value of using positive retrieving to stabilize a dog's emotions is one of the most dramatic benefits of obedience training. Although this novice book gives no instruction on retrieving, nor should it, there are a few facts I should mention so you will not become bogged down with opinions on play versus positive retrieving. The honest owners of dogs trained by play retrieving will admit that their dogs learn that retrieving is no longer a game but is serious business.

Force retrieving, properly taught, is not a

difficult experience for the dog. Unfortunately, there are more unfounded comments made about the activity by the uninformed than anything else that relates to dogs.

I have heard what are apparently nonreaders say my book on Open Obedience, *The Koehler Method of Open Obedience for Ring, Home, and Field*, advocates starting a dog to retrieve by pinching or twisting his ear until the pain causes him to open his mouth. Not so. There is never an intentional twist, and not even a slight pinch, until the dog has shown he understands the command "fetch" by opening his mouth to the dumbbell.

Another common fallacy is that a force-broken retriever doesn't work as happily as one that was trained with play. Such statements seem to be heard less frequently since a young woman offered to bet one hundred dollars per dog that the force-broken dogs would work more happily and more reliably than their play-trained dogs. Although her challenge was widely publicized, there were no takers.

There are various ways to teach responsible retrieving, but I know of no other method than my own, presented in a book, that is guaranteed to work.

The time you spend in developing a positive retriever will be well spent. It can definitely stabilize your dog emotionally, and can be used in many practical ways.

There are many situations where solid obedience can protect a dog and save his master from embarrassment. This benefit is especially important when the dog encounters someone using a wheelchair, a walker, or another piece of equipment. For the dog to shy away from such aids, which have never caused him pain, is to bring pointed stares from observers. Obviously, dogs should be proofed against bad reactions to the sights and sounds of things that are part of everyday life.

Again, the proofing is not a process of glossing over the phony threat with familiarity. It's using responsibility, instilled by obedience training, to provide a real motivation to obey that is stronger than the phony motivation to spook.

When doing a group sit-stay in our obedience classes, we require the dogs to hold the stay while a mower or other noisy implement is pushed along the line a few feet behind the dogs. This is done with the leash attached and stretched out on the ground in front of the dogs so a quick return and correction can be made if any dogs break the stay.

Occasionally, a friend visits us and volunteers to run his wheelchair among the dogs in the class while they are required to do their excercises promptly and accurately. The process continues until all dogs in the line show that their responsibility to stay is stronger than their motivation to shy from the harmless image and noise of an implement.

This reference to an obedience class is merely to indicate that the exercise is well proven. You can work your dog individually without the class environment. But work.

If you have difficulty with your dog holding on the **stand-for-examination,** turn to page 187 and repeat the entire training process the way this book presents it. Read it carefully, and follow it to the letter.

OBEDIENCE COMPETITION

When, under the most distracting conditions, your dog will reliably and accurately perform those exercises that you have taught him, it can be said that he is capable of meeting the standard routine tests that the American Kennel Club uses to accredit a Companion Dog, commonly called a "C.D."

If you have a purebred dog and enjoy competition, you can enter a new field of interest and pleasure by participating in the formal obedience of licensed shows. You and your dog will improve greatly when you face the objective of doing your best for a score.

The problem in "doing your best" is to become familiar with ring handling procedure and the atmosphere of being judged so that you will be smooth and confident in your handling and able to communicate with your dog in a way that brings out his fullest response. Regardless of how obedient his dog is or how much a person has studied the rules and handling demands in books, there are two or more things he must do before he can expect his dog to score well in competition. He should observe, first-hand, the handling of dogs in the obedience ring and get someone to run through the novice routine with him so he will acquire practice in giving the correct commands and properly executing the maneuvers when he is told to do so, instead of hesitating until he feels his position is better adjusted to that of the dog.

In brief summary, the regulations which are of major concern to handling are those that limit a handler to a single command each time the judge orders a test of performance and that demand the handler be penalized for any additional motion or sound, given intentionally or unintentionally, that could possibly give a further cue to the dog. So, if you have any nervous wigglings, head scratchings, or other unusual mannerisms, learn to control them while you're working a dog in the ring. Remember, too, the time and manner of executing the exercises is not left to your initiative. The stops, starts, and patterns of performance must be done when and as the judge specifies. Only by this observation and practice in executing the exercises on another's order will you free yourself from compromise and develop the balance and confidence necessary to get good obedience scores.

Ask the one who runs through the routine with you to watch and listen for any motions or words that would cause you to lose points for double commands and unintentional cues. As an aid to what you observed at ringside, you can get a booklet containing much information from The American Kennel Club, 51 Madison Avenue, New York, N.Y. 10010.

The hard-working judges, who give so much time to obedience, vary somewhat in their interpretation of the rules and the routine patterns to be used for judging, but generally the variations are not of great significance.

Watch the practice matches and novice judging at shows whenever you can. Read your rule book carefully. Practice with someone putting you through the routine, in association with other obedience enthusiasts and their dogs if possible. You'll soon be prepared to complete the requirements, as outlined in your rule book, and you'll get much profit and find a new world of fun and friends in helping your well-trained dog acquire the title of Companion Dog.

With this success, your interest in further training and showing is certain to grow, which is one of the nicest things that could happen to you and your dog.

Because of the uniformity in patterns and judging procedures, the obedience ring provided an excellent facility for comparing and accrediting dogs in the performance of standardized exercises. The opportunity for competition created a new dog-centered activity that flourished as obedience groups and clubs sprang up, and regional and national trials provided a host of honors and awards.

But observers have noticed that as competition grew more intense, the original concept of obedience seemed to be subordinated to the "acts" that would be performed in a ring. The exact uniformity that was needed to accurately compare performance encouraged training that was essentially rehearsals and choreography of the exact and predictable routines.

In an effort to influence judges, some of the routines were embellished by spicing up the patterns with tidbits for the dogs that would be offered in the rehearsals. In these practice sessions, dogs are essentially baited from one point to another so that expectation of food rewards at significant points in the routine would brighten the dogs' work in the ring. Some handlers have gone so far as to carry goodies in their mouths to pattern a dog to hit a spot in the pattern where the ejected morsels were dropped in the rehearsals.

Some otherwise normal individuals are enchanted by dogs that heel along while they look up adoringly at the handler's face. It is now advocated by some that the scoring be modified so that bonus points can be awarded for showmanship.

Most significantly, it is being observed that there is a growing number of dogs that, when not performing their routines in the isolation of the ring, are as unruly at the ringside as dogs that are untrained, pulling on their leashes and even showing aggression to other dogs.

Because of this growing subordination of practical obedience to choreographed ring routines, the format for in-and-out-of-the-ring obedience competition was conceived.

Obedience enthusiasts have an opportunity to do something very worthwhile for dogs and the people who love them by finding ways to encourage the growth of **in-and-out trials.** The following information should be of interest to dog club members or obedience exhibitors in every area of the United States.

The facility needed for an **in-and-out trial** consists of two rings, each the size of an average obedience ring. The rings are placed parallel to each other, about ten feet apart. The ring that is most approachable from the road or parking area is the one that should be used for the distraction corridor.

The distractions can be somewhat varied

according to the components available, but there are five items that are specifically recommended: 1. A goat or sheep, staked about ten feet off the course; 2. A pan of tripe, placed on the ground close to where the dog will pass; 3. A scattering of boiled liver; 4. A ball rolled across the course in front of the dog; 5. A caged chicken or duck. The remaining ten distractions can be chosen from among such things as securely caged small animals or anything that might distract a working obedience dog.

The distractions should be spaced widely enough so the dog will not feel pressured into a solid setup.

A judge will be needed for the distraction corridor and a conventional judge is required for the obedience ring.

The test begins at the point where the handler parks his car and calls his dog, unleashed, to heel. At the moment the dog is on the ground, at free-heel, he will face the first distraction as a decoy dog is led across the path a few feet in front of him. The handler-dog team will then proceed to the distraction ring on a course that will not appear to be significant to the dog, with the dog at free-heel.

They will continue on a course through the ring that exposes the dog to all of the distractions and out the side gate to the gate of the adjacent conventional ring, at which time the handler will stop and attach his leash and enter the ring as directed by the steward.

The dog will then be judged according to the American Kennel Club regulations that apply to the class in which he's competing. The score he receives in the conventional ring will be added to the score he earned in the distraction ring and the composite score will determine the dog's placing in the competition.

Trained dogs are good citizens. *(Photo by C. Lydon Lippincott)*

IN & OUT MATCH

Name _____

Address _____

Zip Code _____ Phone _____

Class Entered _____ Dog's Home _____

Dog's Age _____ Dog's Sex _____

ENTRY FEES: $5.00 per dog   Paid: Amount_____

Check _____ Check No._____Cash_____

(Please make checks payable to Charlynne Kenning)

Note: There is no division of classes.
          Just Novice, Open, and Utility.

If you have a Novice degree, but do not have an
Open degree you may enter the Novice class. If you
have an Open degree, you must enter Open. If you
have a Utility degree, you may enter the Open class.

DISTRACTION SCORING

3 Points: **Extra command to heel**
               Slapping Leg   [
               Whistling   [**(any extra noises, motions)**
               Snapping Fingers [

Zero: **Physically restraining the dog**
               Dog going after cat
               Dog eating food
               Dog playing with any distraction

Total Score Possible: 100 Points

Dog No.	Deductions	Score	Composite Score

1	31	61	91	121	151	181	211	241	271	301	331
2	32	62	92	122	152	182	212	242	272	302	332
3	33	63	93	123	153	183	213	243	273	303	333
4	34	64	94	124	154	184	214	244	274	304	334
5	35	65	95	125	155	185	215	245	275	305	335
6	36	66	96	126	156	186	216	245	276	306	336
7	37	67	97	127	157	187	217	247	277	307	337
8	38	68	98	128	158	188	218	248	278	308	338
9	39	69	99	129	159	189	219	249	279	309	339
10	40	70	100	130	160	190	220	250	280	310	340
11	41	71	101	131	161	191	221	251	281	311	341
12	42	72	102	132	162	192	222	252	282	312	342
13	43	73	103	133	163	193	223	253	283	313	343
14	44	74	104	134	164	194	224	254	284	314	344
15	45	75	105	135	165	195	225	255	285	315	345
16	46	76	106	136	166	196	226	256	286	316	346
17	47	77	107	137	167	197	227	257	287	317	347
18	48	78	108	138	168	198	228	258	288	318	348
19	49	79	109	139	169	199	229	259	289	319	349
20	50	80	110	140	170	200	230	260	290	320	350
21	51	81	111	141	171	201	231	261	291	321	351
22	52	82	112	142	172	202	232	262	292	322	352
23	53	83	113	143	173	203	233	263	293	323	353
24	54	84	114	144	174	204	234	264	294	324	354
25	55	85	115	145	175	205	235	265	295	325	355
26	56	86	116	146	176	206	236	266	296	326	356
27	57	87	117	147	177	207	237	267	297	327	357
28	58	88	118	148	178	208	238	268	298	328	358
29	59	89	119	149	179	209	239	269	299	329	359
30	60	90	120	150	180	210	240	270	300	330	360